WORLD BANK TECHNICAL PAPER NO. 417
Social Challenges of Transition Series

Welfare and the Labor Market in Poland

Social Policy during Economic Transition

Jan J. Rutkowski

The World Bank
Washington, D.C.

Technical Papers are published to communicate the results of the Bank's work to the development community with the least possible delay. The typescript of this paper therefore has not been prepared in accordance with the procedures appropriate to formal printed texts, and the World Bank accepts no responsibility for errors. Some sources cited in this paper may be informal documents that are not readily available.

The findings, interpretations, and conclusions expressed in this paper are entirely those of the author(s) and should not be attributed in any manner to the World Bank, to its affiliated organizations, or to members of its Board of Executive Directors or the countries they represent. The World Bank does not guarantee the accuracy of the data included in this publication and accepts no responsibility for any consequence of their use. The boundaries, colors, denominations, and other information shown on any map in this volume do not imply on the part of the World Bank Group any judgment on the legal status of any territory or the endorsement or acceptance of such boundaries.

The material in this publication is copyrighted. Requests for permission to reproduce portions of it should be sent to the Office of the Publisher at the address shown in the copyright notice above. The World Bank encourages dissemination of its work and will normally give permission promptly and, when the reproduction is for noncommercial purposes, without asking a fee. Permission to copy portions for classroom use is granted through the Copyright Clearance Center, Inc., Suite 910, 222 Rosewood Drive, Danvers, Massachusetts 01923, U.S.A.

ISSN: 0253-7494

Cover: Photos by Nelson Ryland. Art by Joyce Petruzzelli.

Jan J. Rutkowski is a labor economist at the World Bank's resident mission in Poland.

Library of Congress Cataloging-in-Publication Data

Rutkowski, Jan J., 1954–
    Welfare and the labor market in Poland : social policy during
economic transition / Jan J.Rutkowski.
        p.   cm. — (World Bank technical paper, ISSN 0253-7494 ; no.
    417. Social challenges of transition series)
    ISBN 0-8213-4318-1
    1. Income distribution—Poland.   2. Poland—Social policy.
3. Labor market—Poland.   4. Poland—Economic conditions—1990.
5. Public welfare—Poland.   I. Title.   II. Series: World Bank
technical paper ; no. 417.   III. Series: World Bank technical paper.
Social challenges of transition series.
HC340.3.Z9I5167   1998
361.9438—dc21   98-27896
                                                                    CIP

Contents

Forward..vii

Abstract...viii

Acknowledgments...iv

Executive Summary...x

Introduction...1

**Chapter 1: The Withering Away of the Welfare State? Trends in Social
Expenditure during Economic Transition** 5

   The inheritance...5

   Size of the government...7

   Trends in social expenditures...8

   Determinants of social expenditure growth.......................................12

   Pension spending...13

   Summary..16

Chapter 2: Changes in the Labor Market: Emerging Risks and Opportunities.....17

   Introduction: the emergence of labor markets..................................17

   Employment opportunities and the risk of unemployment.....................18

      Education, skills and unemployment..18

      Policy response to unemployment...22

   Changes in the wage structure..26

      Rising wage differentials...26

      Wage developments in the private sector..................................32

      Changing returns to labor market skills....................................35

   Labor market transition: an assessment...41

   Summary..45

Chapter 3: **Distributional Consequences of Transition: The New Rich and the New Poor** 47

    Income inequality...48

        Income composition...48

        Relative incomes 49

        Overall income inequality...52

        Within group inequality..54

        Conclusions on income inequality....................................55

    Poverty and prosperity...57

        Social mobility: in and out of poverty..............................57

        Poverty and the economic growth...................................61

        Can the poor benefit from the trickle down of economic growth? ...62

        Conclusions on poverty and prosperity.............................64

    Inequality, poverty and the policy response.............................64

    Income distribution in Poland vis-à-vis OECD countries............69

        Income inequality in Poland and in OECD countries..........69

        The role and distribution of social transfers 73

    Summary 77

References..79

Statistical Annexes..83

    Annex 1.   Data for figures in chapter 1................84

    Annex 2.   Data for figures in chapter 2................86

    Annex 3.   Data for figures in chapter 3................91

List of Tables

Table 1.1   Social expenditure as percentage of GDP (1989-1995) 8

Table 1.2   Factors of pension expenditure growth in 1989-1995 14

Table 2.1   Labor market prospects by age, gender, education and place
             of residence, 1995 21

Table 2.2   Private and public sector wages by broad occupation, 1995 33

Table 2.3   Earnings differentials by educational attainment (1988 – 1995) 36

Table 2.4   Ratios of earnings of men by educational attainment
             (early 1990s) 39

Table 3.1   Relative incomes (1987 and 1995) 50

Table 3.2   Summary of income distribution (1987 and 1995) 53

Table 3.3   Summary of income distribution by socio-economic group, Percentiles of Median,
             1987 and 1995 55

Table 3.4   Distribution of household members by quintile and socio-
             demographic characteristics of households, 1987 and 1995 58

Table 3.5   Inequality by income components, 1995 65

Table 3.6   Percentage quintile shares by income components, 1995 67

Table 3.7   Concentration and progressivity of social transfers,
             1989 and 1995 68

Table 3.8   Average transfers as a percent of median equivalent income
             by quintile (mid/late 1980s) 75

Table 3.9   Distribution of transfers by quintile (mid/late 1980s) 76

List of Figures

Figure 1.1   Social expenditure as percentage of total public expenditure (1989-1995)...................9

Figure 1.2   Cumulative growth of real expenditures (1989 = 100)..9

Figure 1.3   Social expenditure as percentage of GDP (1989-1995)....................................10

Figure 1.4   Percentage composition of social expenditures, 1995 11

Figure 2.1   Unemployment rates by educational attainment, 1995 18

Figure 2.2   Changes in earnings distribution, 1987 - 1995 27

Figure 2.3   Real wage growth by selected percentiles (1987 =100)...................................28

Figure 2.4   Earnings distribution in CEE countries before and during transition 30

Figure 2.5   Decile ratio in Poland and in selected OECD countries
(late 1980s/early 1990s)..31

Figure 2.6   Incidence of low pay in CEE countries before and during transition 31

Figure 2.7   Incidence of low pay in Poland and in selected OECD countries
(late 1980s/early 1990s)..32

Figure 2.8   Earnings distribution in public and private sectors, 1995....................................33

Figure 2.9   Incidence of low and high pay, 1995..35

Figure 2.10   Earnings differentials by educational attainment
(basic vocational = 100) 38

Figure 2.11   Ratio of top decile earnings of white collar workers to top decile
earnings of blue collar workers by sector, 1987 and 1995...........................40

Figure 2.12   Ratio of average private sector wage to public sector wage by
educational attainment, 1995 (public sector = 100) 41

Figure 3.1   Income composition (1987 and 1995) 49

Figure 3.2   Household incomes relative to average income by socio-economic
group, 1987 and 1995...51

Figure 3.3   Incidence of low and high incomes by educational attainment of
household head, worker households (1988 and 1995)..................................60

Figure 3.4   Composition of income quintiles in 1995 by educational attainment of
household head..61

Figure 3.5   Summary of income distribution in OECD countries in late 1980's:
Gini coefficient 70

Figure 3.6   Summary of income distribution in OECD countries in late 1980's..........................72

Figure 3.7   Percentage distribution of low, modest and high income groups 74

Figure 3.8   The importance and distribution of social benefits by quintile
in Poland (1995) 76

Foreword

In many ways Poland is considered to be a leader among transition economies. It was one of the first countries to adopt dramatic and rapid political and economic reforms in 1990 -- including the package of stabilization, price reform and privatization measures which became the benchmark for 'shock therapy' reforms throughout the region. It was accepted into the OECD in 1997 and is now a leading candidate for accession to the European Union. Because it has become the prototype of shock therapy reformers, Poland provides an excellent case study of the impact of transition policies on the social sectors, and the transformation of the welfare state in general. Many of the trends identified early in the 1990s in Poland, including rising unemployment, widening income distribution and growing poverty have been harbingers of developments throughout the region. Similarly, more recent improvements in unemployment and poverty indicators in Poland may illustrate future trends for neighboring transition economies.

This study explores the dynamics of change in social policy and social welfare in Poland, focusing on trends in labor markets, income distribution and poverty, and policy responses in social assistance and social insurance, as well as health and education. It analyzes policy responses to changes in social welfare, and examines the evolution of the welfare state during transition. In contrast with initial predictions that transition would lead to social outcomes at odds with those in developed countries, the report finds that welfare state developments in Poland are broadly compatible with those observed in Western European OECD countries. Many of the most challenging issues facing policy makers in Poland closely resemble those of their western counterparts -- including strategies for securing the fiscal sustainability of pension systems, targeting of social assistance, and labor market measures for the long term unemployed. Improved understanding of the socioeconomic impact of transition in Poland has salient implications both for neighboring countries in Central and Eastern Europe and the West as well.

This report is another in the Social Challenges of Transition series. Initiated in 1994, the project examines the social opportunities and risks facing people and the policy responses taken by governments since 1989, by monitoring indicators of health, education and labor markets and social protection. The findings contained in the reports make a valuable contribution to our understanding of social developments in the transition economies of Europe and Central Asia and provide a basis for further improvements in the content and quality of our support to the countries in the region.

James Christopher Lovelace
Director
Human Development Sector Unit
Europe and Central Asia Region

Abstract

This report assesses changes in social welfare and policy in Poland during the economic transition. It argues that contrary to prior expectations, during the transition the welfare state has increased rather than diminished. This increase partly reflects the costs of developing a social safety net for the most vulnerable groups, but mainly the increasing generosity of pension benefits. As a result, the Polish social protection system is extremely generous by OECD standards.

While social transfers in Poland account for a substantial part of poor families' income, the bulk of transfers goes to wealthy families and only a small fraction to the poorest. Thus social transfers do not attenuate income inequality, which has increased considerably. This increase has primarily resulted from widening of wage differentials and the emergence of unemployment. However, Poland still remains relatively egalitarian in comparison with OECD countries. Widespread fears of exorbitant income disparities and polarization of society have proved to be exaggerated.

The primary cause of increased income inequality has been the significant increase in returns to human capital. Highly skilled white-collar workers, especially those who found employment in the private sector, have experienced substantial improvement in their relative and absolute incomes. Less-skilled blue-collar workers, who are the majority, have seen their relative income status deteriorate significantly. These workers have yet to gain from private sector employment. On the contrary, for them changing from the public to the private sector usually entails a wage loss.

Acknowledgments

This report was prepared as a part of a larger study on the *Social Challenges of Transition (SCT)*, carried out by the World Bank's Human Development Sector Unit for the Europe and Central Asia Region under the direction of Chris Lovelace, Sector Director and Maureen Lewis, Sector Leader for HD Economics.

The report came from an idea of Ralph W. Harbison, who originated the SCT project. The author is grateful for his continued enthusiasm and support during the writing of the paper.

The study benefited from comments on an earlier draft by the following individuals: Emily Andrews, Luca Barbone, Ralph Harbison, Maureen Lewis, Branko Milanovic, Dena Ringold, and Sandor Sipos. Special thanks are due to Tom Hoopengardner, who served as a peer reviewer. The study benefited greatly from his detailed and thoughtful comments and suggestions. The author would like to thank Dorota Holzer-Zelazewska for her excellent research assistance, Stephanie Faul and Dena Ringold for making substantial editorial improvement to the text. Ian Conachy, projects assistant, provided formatting, graphic and document production assistance.

The author is responsible for the opinions and conclusions reported in the paper, and for any remaining errors.

Executive Summary

This report assesses changes in social welfare and policy that have taken place in Poland during the economic transition. It is part of the Social Challenges of Transition project, which documents and analyzes development trends and patterns that have emerged during the transition in the ECA region.

The empirical study tests the main hypotheses about changes in the role of the welfare state, the workings of the labor market, the distributional consequences of transition, and, more generally, about the winners and losers in the transition.

This analysis produced the following four principal insights:

- Contrary to expectations, the welfare state has increased rather than diminished during the economic transition in Poland. This increase is largely accounted for by the staggering growth of cash social transfers, especially pensions. These cash transfers partly reflect the costs of developing a social safety net, but primarily consist of increasingly generous pension benefits and widespread early retirement. In contrast, expenditures on social services such as education and health care have suffered during the transition. As a result, consumption by social security recipients has taken precedence over investment in human capital.

- The Polish social protection system is extremely generous even by OECD standards. While social transfers account for a substantial part of poor people's income, most transfers go to relatively wealthy families and only a small fraction to the poorest. This results from the generosity of earnings-related pensions, which take most pensioners out of poverty.

- Income inequality has increased considerably during the transition, mainly as a result of growing wage differentials and the emergence of unemployment. Despite this increase, Poland remains a relatively egalitarian society by OECD standards, with a large middle class. Fears of exorbitant income disparities and polarization of society are not supported by empirical evidence. Moreover, notwithstanding rising inequality, the poor have benefited from economic growth. After an initial sharp increase, the incidence and depth of poverty have begun to decline.

- The major driving force behind the increase in income inequality has been a significant increase in returns to human capital, which has emerged as a key factor in determining family living standards. Households headed by well-educated, highly skilled white-collar workers have markedly improved their income status and are prevalent among the wealthy. In contrast, families headed by poorly educated, low-skilled manual workers and farmers have seen their relative income deteriorate. Such households prevail among the poor.

The specific findings are as follows:

The withering away of the welfare state? Trends in social expenditure

Social expenditures now absorb a significantly larger share of the GDP than before the transition. Spending on cash transfers, especially pensions, has risen considerably not only relative to GDP but also in real terms, despite an initial deep fall in the national income. However, spending on social services such as health care and education, while remaining roughly stable as a share of GDP, has suffered from the recession and has fallen in real terms.

Social spending is extremely high in Poland, given a relatively low GDP and high development needs. Exorbitant social transfers have crowded out resources that could otherwise be used for investment and thus are likely to impede economic growth. Reforming the social protection system to enhance its efficiency is therefore a matter of the highest priority. Successful reform should free resources for investment, including investment in human capital, to raise productivity and improve prospects for growth..

Spending on pensions is the single largest component of social expenditure. Poland has one of the most costly public pension systems in Central and Eastern Europe. These high pension costs result mainly from a generous system and plentiful opportunities for early retirement, but also from lax eligibility conditions for disability pensions. Thus reform must have these major objectives: to reduce the generosity of the public pension system, restrict eligibility and create disincentives for early retirement, and restrict eligibility for disability pensions.

Contrary to early expectations, the costs resulting from the emergence of unemployment and poverty in the wake of economic restructuring have not been the major factor behind the rise in social expenditures. Instead, the causes has been skyrocketing pension costs. This remains true even after taking into account that some pensions were substituted for unemployment benefits through early safety-net programs. The increase in cash transfers has been far greater than would be required by unemployment.

The composition of social spending has also changed markedly. The government has shifted resources from in-kind expenditures, such as education and health care, to cash expenditures, such as pensions and social assistance. Given that this shift implies higher present consumption at the cost of lower investment in human capital, it may have detrimental consequences for long-term economic growth.

Changes in the labor market: emerging risks and opportunities

A more liberal labor market has remarkably increased returns to human capital. Well-educated workers have high earnings and face a low risk of unemployment. In contrast, poorly educated workers face a high risk of job loss and, if unemployed, find it difficult to find new jobs. Those who are employed are often poorly paid, especially if they work in the private sector.

Inadequate human capital (the "skill gap") is a significant cause of unemployment in Poland. Roughly speaking, one unemployed worker in seven cannot find a job because he does not have the education employers require. Given that skill mismatches may exist within educational categories, this is a lower-bound estimate of the size of the problem.

Active labor-market policies in Poland vary in their impact on equalizing employment opportunities. Subsidized employment programs tend to enhance the equality of labor-market outcomes by providing jobs to disadvantaged groups. On the other hand, labor-market training is largely received by groups with already high competitive capacity (i.e., the well educated), making opportunity differences even larger.

Although subsidized employment programs seem well targeted, they are not very effective in putting the unemployed back to work. Success rates – defined as the proportion of program participants who find regular jobs – are relatively low. Even program participants themselves do not view the programs as helpful in finding regular work. While the job accession rate for ex-trainees is significantly higher than for participants in subsidized employment programs, this partly reflects selection bias: Training participants tend to have more favorable personal attributes than other workers. The allocation of resources between programs and program design can be improved so as to enhance both equity and efficiency.

Earnings dispersion has increased during the transition. The increase has been significant, though it is modest in comparison with that of other transitional economies. At present the level of wage inequality in Poland is similar to that observed in medium to high-inequality OECD countries.

The increase in wage dispersion has been largely caused by changes at the upper end of the earnings distribution. Highly paid workers have become more numerous and their earnings have substantially improved compared to the median worker. Changes at the lower end have been less pronounced. While low-paid workers have become more numerous, their relative earnings status has not deteriorated significantly.

Wage differentials in the private sector are significantly greater than in the public sector. The private sector offers better earnings opportunities for highly skilled workers but pays relatively low wages for less-skilled workers, and many private sector jobs are low-paying jobs. Thus, the well-educated and highly skilled minority has an incentive to seek private-sector employment, but the majority of workers – those with blue-collar or lower-level skills – are better off sticking to the public sector.

The increase in wage differentials has been largely driven by a substantial increase in returns to education and white-collar skills. Well educated white-collar workers have seen a marked improvement in their earnings, while low- skilled blue-collar workers' relative (and often absolute) wages have fallen.

The high incidence of unemployment among low-skilled workers points to insufficient wage adjustment as a possible source of unemployment among this group. The wages of low-skilled workers relative to the median are high in Poland compared to countries with more flexible wage structures.

Distributional consequences of the transition: the new rich and the new poor

The transition in Poland has brought about a substantial increase in the importance of transfer income. Families are now more dependent on income support from the state than they were before the transition. This is coupled with a decline in market income as a share of total income.

Income inequality has increased. Although this increase is quite substantial, it has been relatively modest compared with the experience of many other transitional economies. The current level of inequality is also moderate by transitional economies' standards.

Inequality in Poland has been driven largely by rising prosperity rather than growing impoverishment. Some families have seen a considerable improvement in their relative income that has not been accompanied by a significant worsening of the income status of the poor.

Those who have gained from the changes in income distribution are outnumbered by those who have lost. However, while the gains have been quite significant, the losses have been rather small.

Inequality has increased not only between social groups but also within groups. Within each socioeconomic group a stratum has emerged (varying from 10 to 30 percent) that has taken advantage of opportunities created by the transition and markedly improved its income.

Families with a high level of human capital now face a much greater opportunity for high income and much lower risk of low income. The opposite is true in the case of families with a low level of human capital. Thus, the "new rich" are the families of well-educated, highly skilled white-collar workers and entrepreneurs. The new poor are the families of poorly educated, low-skilled blue-collar workers and farmers.

Economic growth has begun to trickle down to the poor. It has somewhat reduced the incidence and depth of poverty. This implies that the growth of aggregate income has eventually prevailed over the growth in income inequality.

Public transfers mitigate market-generated inequality but only to a limited degree. This equalizing role is played exclusively by the family allowance and the unemployment benefit, as pensions tend to increase the overall degree of inequality. The transition has changed income distribution so that it has come to resemble that prevailing in middle-inequality European countries, particularly Germany. It seems therefore that the widespread perception of a sharply rising wealth gap in Poland is the result of indeed profound social changes and to a much lesser extent of actual income disparities.

In comparison with the OECD countries, Poland offers an extremely generous social protection system. The part played by transfers in supporting family income in Poland is unmatched by any OECD country except Sweden.

Poland resembles Anglo-Saxon OECD countries in that the share of transfers in family income is high in low-income groups and declines as income increases. But it is very different from Anglo-Saxon OECD countries with regard to the distribution of transfers. In Poland, most social transfers go to the highest-income group and only a small fraction to the bottom. In contrast, in Anglo-Saxon countries transfers tend to be heavily targeted at the poor. The pattern of transfer distribution prevailing in Poland is similar to that observed in France and Italy, where earnings-related pensions also constitute a large part of public payments.

Introduction

The democratization and economic transition that followed the collapse of the communist regime in Poland has brought about dramatic changes. While people have gained freedoms they did not enjoy under the authoritarian regime, they have lost a sense of security. Where they were used to the "cradle-to-grave" protection offered by the communist state, they must now become self-reliant and take responsibility for their own lives.

Market-oriented reforms have created new opportunities as well as new risks. Workers accustomed to lifetime employment and stable earnings now must compete for jobs and wages. Some have adapted to the new environment, taken up the challenge, and seized emerging opportunities. Others have found it difficult to adjust and are suffering from the transition. Market rewards for different skills have changed, as has the income status of different social groups; as a result some who enjoyed a relatively high standard of living under the old system have seen their incomes fall, while others have found prosperity. The transition intensified the struggle for income and introduced new players, such as entrepreneurs, managers in private firms, and recipients of social assistance. It also increased the stakes; income distribution has widened. Under the old regime, the majority of families clustered in the middle and the distance between poverty and prosperity was slight. Now the middle is shrinking and classes of new poor and new rich are emerging. Poverty and prosperity now seem worlds apart.

This increased sense of insecurity and emerging risk has pressured the state to maintain or even enhance its role as an insurer and to develop an adequate social safety net. Many people – mainly those with lower competitive capacity – expect the state to provide old-age security, create jobs, insure against unemployment, prevent excessive income disparities, deliver health care, and assure free access to education. At the same time there is a conviction – largely among the most successful – that the welfare state has to be curbed and that people have to take more responsibility for their lives. These market-oriented elite expect the state to play a subsidiary role and not create perverse incentives by altering market outcomes. The state has tried to redefine its new role among these conflicting expectations, but its ability to transform itself is constrained by voter preferences.

This report documents and analyzes changes in social welfare during the transition in Poland. It tries to identify winners and losers, those who have taken advantage of new opportunities and improved their economic welfare and those who have failed to do so and seen their welfare deteriorate. The report also attempts to identify policies driving the observed changes in welfare[1]

---

[1]   The caveat is that in many instances attributing a given social outcome to a particular policy can prove difficult. Usually, social outcomes are a result of a multitude of different factors and unambiguously disentangling which particular action caused a particular effect may prove close to impossible. For example,

and examines policy responses to emerging challenges of unemployment, income inequality, and poverty.

The analysis is based on empirical evidence, which in many cases is new and unique. The main data sources are two microdata sets: the Labor Force Survey and the Household Budget Survey. Whenever possible, the changes in social welfare in Poland are put into a comparative perspective. First, we compare changes in Poland to those in other transitional economies, using the World Bank's Social Challenges of Transition (SCT) database. We try to establish which social changes are common to transition and which are specific to Poland. Second, we compare social outcomes in Poland to those of developed market economies of OECD countries in order to determine the social structure toward which Poland is steering.

The report reviews changes in three areas of social welfare: state provision of cash benefits and social services (Chapter 1); the workings of the labor market (Chapter 2); and income distribution (Chapter 3).

Chapter 1 addresses the question of whether the transition is associated with the withering away of the welfare state built under the communist regime, as some observers claim. Even if the notion of "state desertion" seems exaggerated, it is reasonable to assume that social spending – high during the socialist period – would be substantially reduced during marketization of the economy. Analysis of trends in social expenditure does not support this hypothesis. Contrary to prior expectations, social expenditures as a share of GDP (a measure of the size of the welfare state) have not decreased, but have grown during the transition.

Important changes have occurred in the composition of social expenditures. Social transfers have increased sharply both in real terms and as a share of GDP, and have crowded out expenditures on social services such as education and health care. This growth of the welfare state is a result of demand for income security and free access to social services. However, the welfare state in Poland has reached its limits and curtailing it has become crucial for long-term growth prospects.

Many of the changes in social welfare have their source in the labor market. In the wake of economic liberalization, employment and wages began to be determined by the interplay of supply and demand rather than administrative fiat. Especially in the growing private sector, the rules of setting wage and employment levels have become virtually the same as in mature market economies. This has had two key welfare consequences: the emergence of large-scale unemployment and the substantial widening of earnings differentials. Unemployment implies new competition for jobs and is a source of growing income inequality. Rising earnings differentials are another source of inequality.

---

we may with great confidence claim that an increase in spending on pensions was the result of government consciously and purposefully increasing the replacement ratio. But it is much more difficult to single out a policy (or a set of policies) that caused high unemployment or an increase in income inequality. Similarly, we cannot unambiguously attribute, say, the deterioration in health status to failure of the health care system. There are many other factors that affect a population's health , such as lifestyle and environmental conditions. Government action is only one of them, and moreover has uncertain impact and significance.

Chapter 2 examines these changes in employment prospects and in the wage structure. Specifically, it concentrates on the labor market prospects of different worker groups. Which groups see the changes that have been occurring in the labor market as an opportunity and which as a peril? Which worker groups benefit from the changes and which lose? In answering these questions emphasis is placed on the role of human capital as a determinant of labor market outcomes. Returns to education and skills were traditionally low under central planning. As expected, the transition brought about a significant increase in the premium on education. Now high skills pay off while low skills often lead to joblessness or low earnings. This is especially the case in the developing private sector. Highly skilled workers have a strong incentive to seek private sector jobs, while low-skilled workers are better off sticking to public-sector jobs.

New patterns of social spending and liberalization of the labor market have contributed to far-reaching changes in income distribution. The conventional wisdom is that the transition in Poland has fostered the rise of a narrow elite and impoverished the rest of society. Some observers claim that income inequalities have reached a magnitude that far exceeds that observed in West European societies, while others point to the polarization of Polish society. Critics also say that the state does not care about the poor, who are left out of economic growth. Chapter 3 analyzes distributional consequences of the transition and tests the validity of these claims.

By and large, these fears are not supported by the evidence. Although income inequality has indeed increased considerably, a comparison of income distribution in Poland with that in the OECD countries shows that Poland remains relatively egalitarian, with a large middle class. Moreover, the poor have begun to reap the benefits of economic growth and the incidence and depth of poverty have stared to fall. However, there is incipient danger that an underclass will emerge whose members cannot find productive employment because of poor human capital, a lack of motivation to work, or alcohol abuse.

The Withering Away Of The Welfare State? Trends In Social Expenditure During Economic Transition

The inheritance

Poland, like other countries in Central and Eastern Europe (CEE), entered transition with a relatively well-developed system of social protection that served the needs of a centrally planned economy. There was state insurance for all major social risks such as old age, disability, sickness, and maternity, as well as a system of universal family allowances. Social services - education and health care - were publicly financed and delivered. On top of this, the state (or state-owned enterprises) financed cultural activities and recreation, while housing and some "priority" consumption goods were heavily subsidized. Social expenditures were correspondingly high, accounting for more than one-fifth of GDP. This figure resembled OECD levels but was substantially larger than in countries at a comparable level of economic development.

The welfare system developed under the centrally planned economy was neither designed nor prepared to fit the needs of a market economy. Most notably, the system was ill-equipped to deal with the emerging problems of mass unemployment and growing poverty. Thus, the need emerged to develop a social safety net that granted income support or employment opportunities to those without sufficient income. This obviously placed growing pressures on the fiscal system, especially given a shrinking tax base caused by unemployment and enterprise insolvency. On the other hand, the government dramatically reduced its spending on subsidies, making it possible to redirect some budgetary resources to finance labor market programs and social assistance.

Apart from an obvious financial aspect, changes in the scope of the welfare state have important political economy implications. Citizens in CEE countries, including Poland, were used to a high level of social protection. Social expenditures were distributed relatively evenly across income groups, giving everybody a stake in the system. High levels of social security and welfare were perceived as a universal citizen right (Milanovic, 1995). Market-oriented reforms have introduced a widespread sense of insecurity. Citizens accustomed to universal welfare found the prospect of reducing the welfare state to a social safety net for the poor worrisome. There has been a sense that the socialist welfare state is withering away.

The prevailing view that the state has a dominant role in welfare provision limits policy choices. Opinion polls show that the public has high expectations of the state and its responsibility for meeting their various needs. Almost one-half the respondents expect the state to provide child care, 50 percent think that the state should guarantee housing for young couples, 80 percent believe that the state is responsible for making jobs available, and up to 90 percent think that the state should guarantee decent pensions. Needless to say, the vast majority considers it the state's duty to provide free education and health care. Tellingly, these views on state responsibility do not vary with respondents' educational attainment, income status, or political orientation (Ferge, 1995).

Thus, the needs and demand for a welfare state are high. The transition itself gave rise to new needs as new risks – such as unemployment and poverty – emerged. A social safety net had to be built to provide income support for the unemployed and low-income families and to ensure the political viability of the reforms. This was especially important given strong political pressure – coming from both the political left and right – to maintain the state's involvement in providing social protection and a wide scope of generous social security benefits.

This pressure for greater state involvement seems to be all the stronger because of the popular perception of "state desertion," or withering away of the socialist welfare state. Some critics believe that during the transition the state has ducked many of its responsibilities, including the provision of basic social services such as health , education, and income support for the needy. Many believe that the state no longer does what it used to do and what it should do.

There are painful trade-offs between short-term investment in safety nets and long-term investment in growth and human resources (Krumm, et al., 1994). Since resources are limited, excessive spending on safety nets can deplete the investible resources for growth. Given that the Polish level of public spending in general and social spending in particular is high relative to GDP, revenues are correspondingly high and likely to be distortionary. The marginal personal income tax rate accounts for 45 percent and payroll taxes to finance social insurance benefits account for even more (48.5 percent). These high rates are likely to diminish labor supply and demand and to encourage the development of an informal economy, reducing the tax base. The bottom line is that the opportunity costs of devoting resources to transfers are considerable and cannot be ignored.

Thus, on the one hand, policy makers are faced with considerable needs and a strong demand for increases in social spending. On the other they face fiscal constraints and high opportunity costs of allocating resources to social transfers. The following analysis focuses on actual policy responses to the needs, demands, and tradeoffs in order to discern government preferences in allocating resources for social purposes. It examines whether the notions of "state desertion" are supported by empirical evidence.

It turns out that the welfare state, large under communism, has become even larger during the transition to a market economy. The increase in the generosity of the social welfare budget has been driven primarily by increased spending on pensions, while spending on social services has decreased. The growth in pension spending has overshadowed what was assumed to be the major focus of the social welfare budget during the transition, namely a social safety net to protect vulnerable groups from emerging risks. The rest of this chapter documents these trends and patterns. It analyses changes in the size of the government, the composition of social expenditure, and factors underlying the growth in social spending.

Size of the government

A basic variable for analyzing changes in social expenditure is the size of the government. The ratio of general government spending to GDP is one measure of the government's involvement in the economy. In the 1980s under central planning, public spending in Poland accounted for 43 to 47 percent of GDP (Rutkowski, 1991). It would be reasonable to assume that the dismantling of central planning would lead to a diminishing role of the state in the economy and a lower share of public spending in the GDP. This has not been the case (Table 1.1). Public spending as a share of GDP has risen dramatically, presently exceeding 50 percent. The big government of a centrally planned economy has become even bigger in the course of transition to a market economy. It has also become big in comparison to OECD countries, let alone market economies at similar levels of economic development.

In explaining this paradox it is important to understand that the growth in public spending as a share of GDP took place during a period of falling output and when GDP was below its pre-transition level.[2] In such a situation the government may tend to protect some merit goods (such as education and health care) against deteriorating economic conditions. But this seems to be a minor part of the story. The major factor accounting for the growth of public expenditures seems to be a sharp rise in social transfers. It is striking that the amount by which the share of public expenditures in GDP increased equals the amount by which the ratio of social transfers to GDP increased. Hence, the increase in public spending was caused largely by the increase in social transfers, specifically pensions. Public expenditure have grown because the welfare state has changed and grown.

The increase in government size that occurred in Poland during economic liberalization is not exceptional among transitional economies. Similar increases in spending ratios occurred in other Central European countries, including the leaders of transition (Barbone and Polackova, 1996). These changes have been driven mainly by what Barbone and Polackova call "social demand," and more generally by the transition from authoritarian to representative government, which tends to strengthen the effective demand for social goods. Social demand becomes a driving force in determining public spending in countries where – as in Poland – there has been no significant involvement of the private sector in meeting the demand for social protection.[3]

---

[2]   Although the ratio has not declined once the GDP recovered.

[3]   By contrast, in some countries -- most notably in Baltics -- the size of the government has been reduced as a result of explicit government priorities, including a forceful move towards new, fully funded pension schemes. Other countries (mainly FSU) saw the drop in public expenditure largely as a result of financial constraints (Barbone and Polackova, 1996).

Table 1.1   Social expenditures as percentage of GDP, 1989-1995

	1989	1992 net c)	1992 gross	1995
Total social expenditures	16.7	28.4	31.5	32.4
Social expenditures in cash	9.0	18.1	20.4	21.4
Social insurance benefits a)	8.9	15.4	17.5	17.6
Pensions	6.5	12.5	14.6	15.6
Benefits a)	2.4	2.8	2.9	1.9
Social assistance and Unemployment benefit	0.1	2.7	2.9	3.9
Social assistance	0.1	1.1	1.1	2.0
Unemployment benefit b)	0.0	1.6	1.7	1.8
Social expenditures in kind	7.7	10.3	11.1	11.0
Education	4.1	5.0	5.4	5.4
Health and social welfare	3.6	5.0	5.3	5.2
Active labor market programs	0.0	0.3	0.3	0.4
Memorandum:				
Public expenditures as percent of GDP	39.9	-	51.8	51.5

- Data not available

| Break in the series

Note: Until 1992 social expenditures are net of personal income tax, since 1992 they are gross social expenditures.

a) Including family allowances
b) Including social security contributions paid on behalf of the unemployed
c) Author's estimates

Source: Statistical Yearbooks, various years. Author's calculations.

Trends in social expenditures

Social expenditures in Poland are growing as a share of public expenditures.[4] Between 1989 and 1995, social expenditures as a share of total public expenditure rose by a remarkable 20 percentage points to 63 percent (Figure 1.1). While the increase in the share of social expenditures in kind has been modest (2 percentage points), the increase in expenditures in cash was indeed impressive (19 percentage points). This is mainly accounted for by the growth in expenditures on social assistance and unemployment benefits, and by the growth of expenditures on pensions, which currently account for almost one-third of all public expenditures.

Social expenditure increased not only as a share of total government spending but also, and even more importantly, in real terms. This increase has been achieved despite the initial deep fall in output. While output in 1995 was about 10 percent below 1989 levels, social expenditures were about 20 percent higher (Figure 1.2). Admittedly, the positive growth in total social expenditure is accounted for by the sharp growth in the real value of

---

[4]   Social expenditures (spending) are expenditures on a social safety net (social protection). Social expenditures in cash are expenditures on benefits (social transfers), which provide income support for individuals in the form of cash. Social expenditures in kind are expenditures on benefits which are provided free of charge in the form of services such as health care, education, and employment services.

expenditures in cash (over 6 percent per annum), whereas the real value of expenditures in kind has fallen in line with the drop in output (a cumulative fall of 12 percent). However, the growth of expenditures in cash has been uneven. While pension spending has grown rapidly, the real value of other cash benefits has tapered off.

Figure 1.1.   Social expenditures as percentage of total public expenditure, 1989-1995

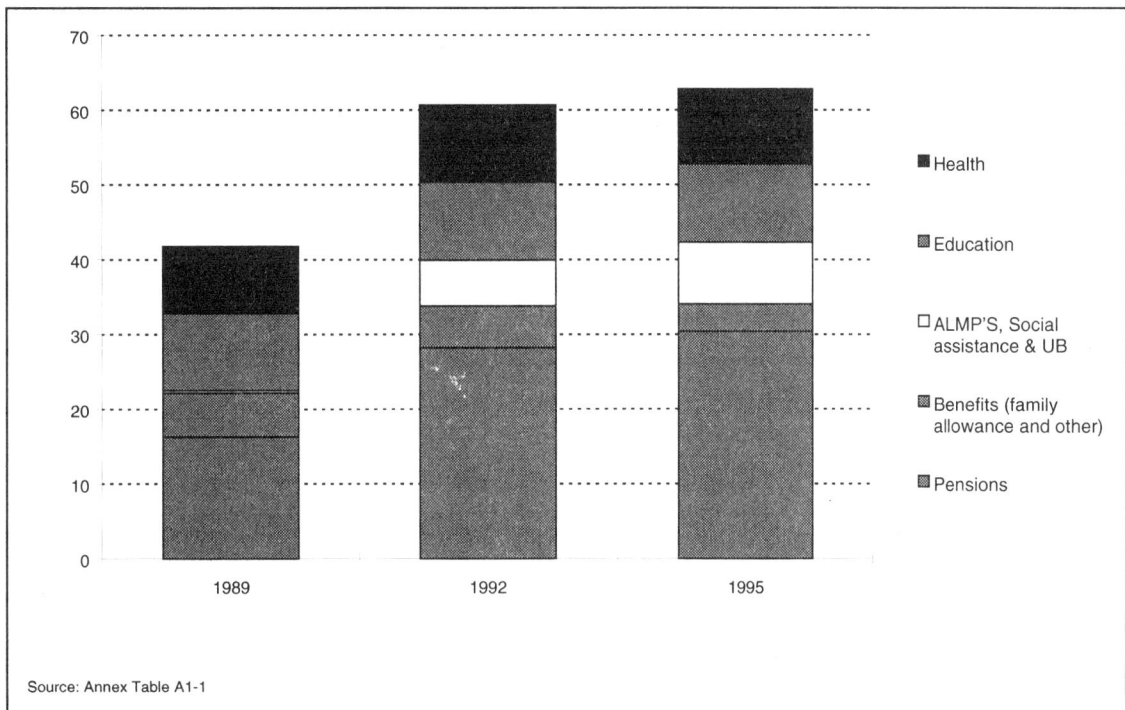

Source: Annex Table A1-1

Figure 1.2   Cumulative growth of real expenditures (1989 = 100)

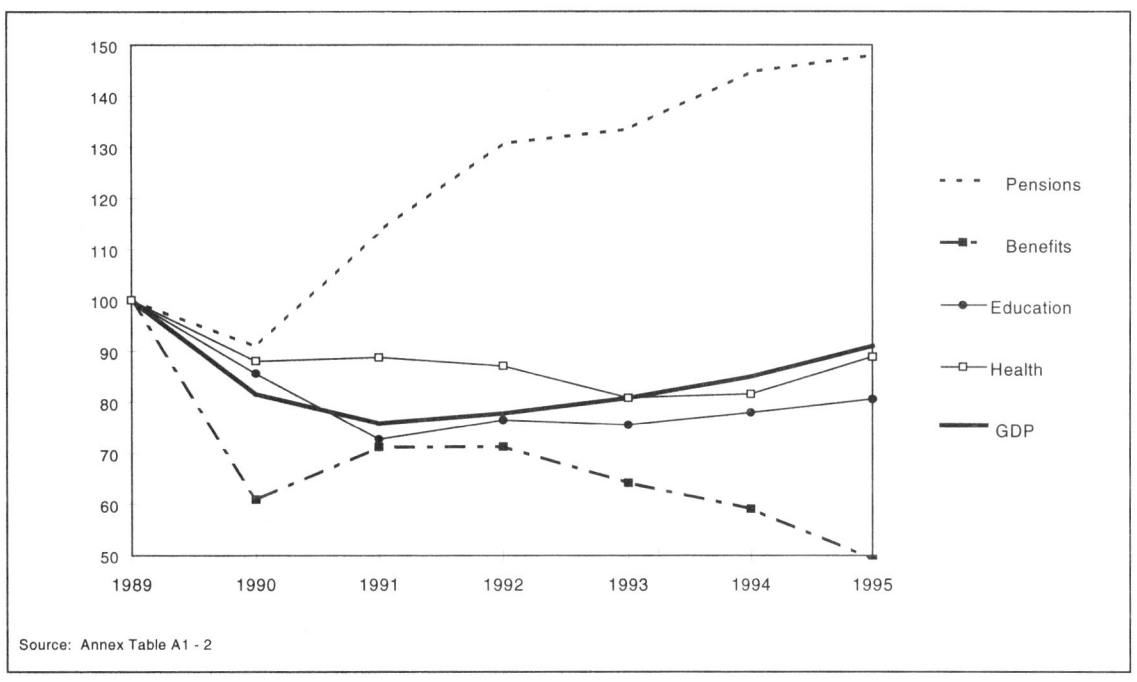

Source: Annex Table A1 - 2

As a result of the rapid growth, social expenditures now account for a substantially larger share of GDP than before the transition (Table 1.1 and Figure 1.3). At present, almost one-third of GDP is allocated to social purposes, up from less than one-fifth in 1989. Social expenditures in cash account for 21 percent of GDP (of which 16 percent goes to pensions), while social expenditures in kind account for 11 percent of GDP. Social expenditures in cash relative to GDP are now twice as large as in 1989, while social expenditures in kind remained roughly stable.

This picture of soaring social spending should be accompanied by two caveats. First, conventionally defined social expenditures do not cover an important element of the communist welfare state, namely, subsides to consumer goods. In all centrally planned economies consumer subsidies were widespread and spending on them was high relative to GDP. In the course of price liberalization and market reforms, subsides have been dramatically reduced. In Poland, subsides to consumer goods as a share of GDP fell from about 9 percent in the late 1980s to 3 percent in the early years of transition. Some portion of the increase in cash social transfers can be thus regarded as compensation for the repeal of consumer subsides, a "monetization of social transfers." However, even if the switch from subsidies to cash transfers is accounted for, the basic picture of escalating social spending remains intact.

The second point is more technical. A portion of the increase in social expenditures results from the introduction of personal income tax in 1992. Accordingly, until 1992 expenditures on pensions, for example, were expenditures on *net* pensions. Since 1992 they have been expenditures on *gross* pensions – *net* pensions plus the personal income tax. If this change is taken into account then the increase of social expenditures as a share of GDP is smaller by some 3 percentage points. Again, this does not change the overall picture of a strong increase in social spending.

Figure 1.3   Social expenditures as percentage of GDP, 1989-1995

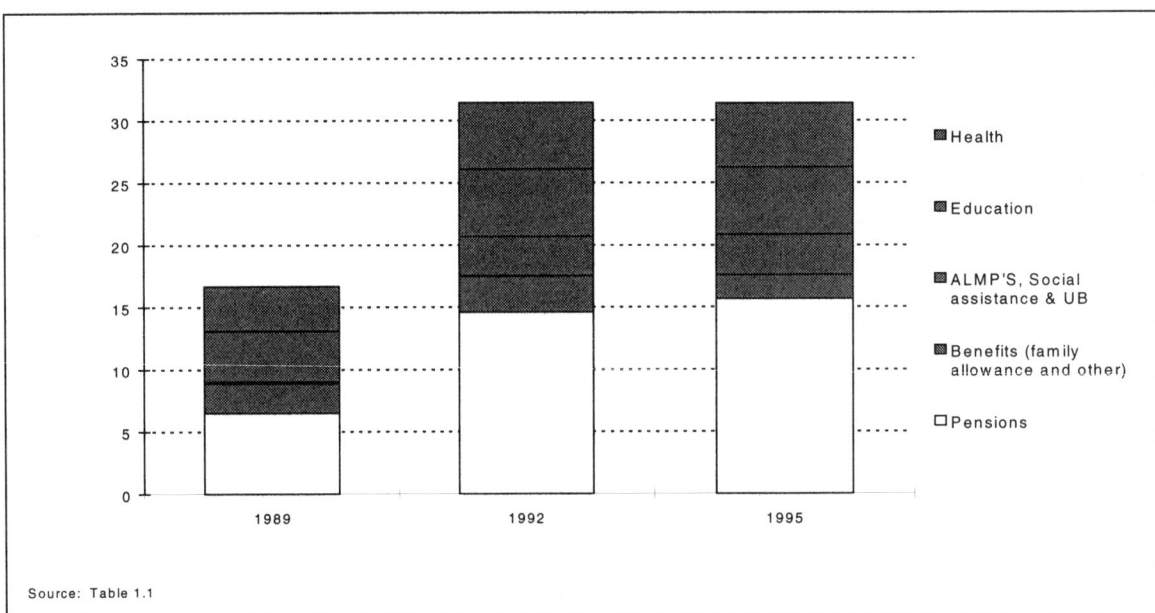

Source: Table 1.1

It is usually assumed that the goods the government buys, among them social security, education, and health, are luxury goods.[5] Accordingly, as societies grow richer they buy proportionately more of them (Abizadeh, 1988). This is reflected in the Wagner's Law of the rising share of government expenditures. If the income elasticity of demand for government expenditures is indeed greater than unity, then it is expected that a fall in the national income should be associated with a declining share of public spending.

The economic adjustment period in Poland has not conformed to this rule. Social expenditures, especially in cash, have proved to be highly protected and rose in real terms despite a falling GDP. Even education and health expenditures have been protected as a share of GDP, although the real value of expenditures in these sectors has declined. This is in contrast to the experience of many adjusting countries where the share of social services in the public budget and GDP has tended to decline (Kakwani et al., 1990; Noss, 1991). Thus, social expenditure, both in cash and in kind, has been protected relative to the rest of the government budget and to GDP.

Figure 1.4   Percentage composition of social expenditures, 1995

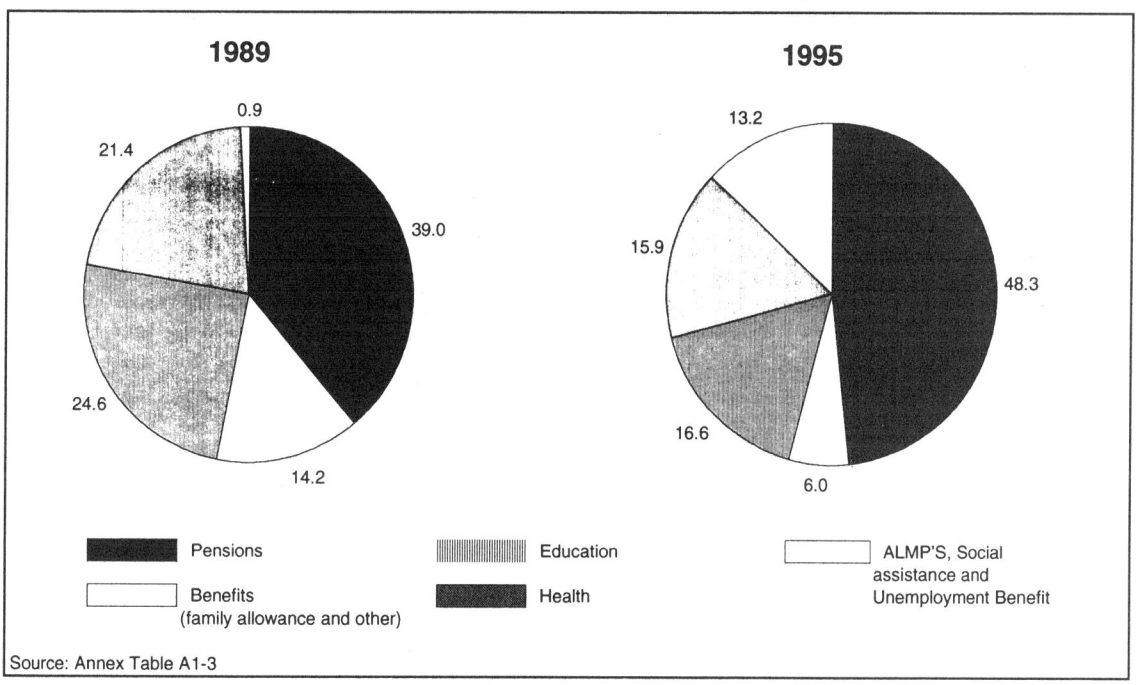

Source: Annex Table A1-3

Far-reaching changes have taken place in the composition of social expenditures, reflecting changing priorities within the government (Figure 1.4). The most visible has been the shift from expenditures in kind to expenditures in cash. At present social expenditures in cash account for two-thirds of total social expenditures, up from just over one-half in 1989.

---

5   They are luxury goods in the sense that their income elasticity tends to be greater than one, which is a condition stronger than that for a normal good (income elasticity greater than zero). Thus, luxury goods are goods such that more income means not only higher consumption but also consumption proportionally higher than that of other ("necessary") goods.

The most important single item is pensions, which account for almost one-half of all social expenditures (an almost 10 percentage point increase) and more than 70 percent of cash expenditures. Correspondingly, growing pension spending has crowded out other cash benefits. The new items, expenditures on labor markets and social assistance, absorb about one-tenth of total social expenditure, translating into 3.2 percent of GDP. This last figure approximates the financial burden caused by emerging unemployment and poverty.[6]

Opponents of economic liberalization claim that the transition destroyed the welfare system inherited from communism. Some observers criticize the present approach toward government as open or hidden "state desertion" (Eatwell et al., 1995). In the light of the presented evidence, these claims appear exaggerated. Almost two-thirds of all general government spending and almost one third of GDP now go to social purposes. However, the Polish experience is not unique. Similar trends have occurred in other transition economies, including Hungary, Bulgaria, Slovakia, and – to a lesser extent – the Czech Republic. This led Sachs (1995) to conclude that "... most East Europeans want both a market economy and the security of an extensive social safety net."

What then are the roots of the perception of state desertion? There are several possible answers. First, the rhetoric of free markets and arguments for circumscribing the role of the state in a market society are often mistaken for reality. Second, change and its associated insecurity lead to the feeling that traditional social security institutions have been dismantled and not been replaced by new ones. Third, the growing share of privately provided services, such as education and health, mirrored by a declining share of state-provided services, may create the impression that the state has dodged its responsibility for providing social goods. And last, but not least, what people experience is the absolute amount and quality of services delivered rather than the economic definition of the size of the welfare state (i.e., social expenditures relative to GDP). Spending on social services is irrelevant if quality and access deteriorate. In this sense, the socialist welfare state indeed diminished during the transition, but mainly as a result of the contraction in output rather than as a result of the state deliberately withdrawing from financing of social services.

Determinants of social expenditure growth

The very fact that social expenditures have been protected during the transition is not in itself necessarily a positive development. A proper evaluation of this trend requires an identification of the underlying reasons for the growth and the comparison – at least qualitatively – of associated costs and benefits.

Two major factors have contributed to the growth of social spending relative to government budget and GDP. First and most important is the growth in pension expenditure, which added 9 percent of GDP to total social expenditure. The second factor is the growth in expenditure on social assistance and unemployment benefits, which added over 4 percent of GDP.

---

[6] The social cost of unemployment – the forgone output – is of course much greater than the cost of policies to alleviate unemployment.

Apparently, these are two different factors. The growth in expenditure on social assistance and unemployment benefits has been a response to growing poverty and unemployment and has been crucial to the reforms' political viability. Public resources have been transferred to groups whose material well-being has deteriorated directly in the wake of economic restructuring, such as the jobless. In this sense, these expenditures are a necessary cost of market-oriented reforms. The growth in pension expenditures is of a different nature. Much of it results from a substantial increase in the level of pensions relative to previous earnings (the replacement rate). Thus, additional public resources have been transferred to maintain or raise the welfare of groups who have not been directly affected by economic restructuring.

However, the rise in pension spending has been also caused by a sharp increase in the number of pensioners. This increase resulted from the government's policy to encourage early retirement of redundant workers by relaxing pension rules. Workers induced to retire early were granted higher pensions benefit rather than lower unemployment compensation benefit. Thus, political economy considerations substituted pensions for unemployment benefits. A part of the increase in expenditures on pensions reflects the financial costs of unemployment, which blurs the line between pension spending and spending on social assistance and unemployment benefits. Nonetheless, the point remains valid that the rise in pension expenditures overshadowed the increase in expenditures on unemployment benefits and social assistance. This is noteworthy, since a common a priori assumption was that the costs resulting from emerging unemployment and poverty would dominate other types of social transfers.

Pension spending

Usually an increase in pension spending results from an aging population. Table 1.2 documents that this has not been the case in Poland. The increase in the population of pensionable age during the early 1990s was modest and the increase in the old-age dependency ratio was negligible. Clearly, demographic factors were not the driving force behind soaring pension expenditures. A much greater change occurred in the number of pension beneficiaries relative to the number of contributors, that is, in the system dependency ratio. From 1989 to 1995, the number of pensioners went up by one-third, of which the number of recipients of old-age pensions increased by 40 percent and the number of recipients of disability pensions by 33 percent. Correspondingly, the system dependency ratio rose dramatically, from 40 in 1989 to 59 in 1995. Although it is pretty clear that the major cause of rapid pension expenditure growth has been an increase in the number of pensioners, this is not the only significant factor. A substantial rise in the earnings replacement ratio[7] – from 53 percent to 74 percent in the case of old-age pensions – has added to the pension burden.

As noted, the dramatic growth in the number of pensioners was a reaction to growing unemployment and shrinking earnings opportunities. Workers were granted special early

---

[7]   Ratio of average pension to average earnings.

retirement options or disability entitlements to encourage them to leave their jobs without joining the ranks of the unemployed (Andrews and Rashid, 1996). Firms were encouraged to pension off older workers, rather than to lay off prime-age workers.[8]

Table 1.2   Factors of pension expenditure growth in 1989-1995

	1989	1995	Average annual growth rate
	in '000s		in percent
Population, total	38038	38609	0.2
Population of working age a)	21889	22647	0.6
Employment	17130	15325	-1.8
Population of pensionable age b)	4799	5317	1.7
Number of pensioners, total	6827	9085	4.9
Old age	3214	4488	5.7
Disability	2551	3391	4.9
Worker system			
Number of pensioners	5471	7036	4.3
Old age	2264	3230	6.1
Disability	2152	2629	3.4
Farmer system			
Number of pensioners	1356	2049	7.1
Old age	950	1258	4.8
Disability	399	762	11.4
Ratios (in percent)			
Old-age dependency ratio c)	21.9	23.5	x
System dependency ratio d)	39.9	59.3	x
Replacement rate e, f)			
All pensions	47.9	64.1	x
Old-age pensions	53.3	74.1	x

x Not applicable

a) 18-64 for men, 18-59 for women

b) 65+ for men, 60+ for women

c) Population of pensionable age/Population of working age

d) Number of pensioners/Employment (number of contributors)

e) Average gross pension benefit/Average gross earnings

f) Worker system

Source: Statistical Yearbooks, various years. Author's calculations.

Early retirement appealed to older workers for two reasons: First, early retirement become less costly to workers. Those who accepted early retirement did not lose much of their pension since the existing formula does not sufficiently   penalize early retirement (especially given the large increase in the replacement rate). Second, given that workers can

---

[8]   From the point of view of the labor market, it is reasonable to pension off older workers with obsolete skills who are very hard to retrain. The problem is that in Poland this was done in too high numbers and at too high a cost per pensioner.

combine their pension benefits with earned wages, early retirement can increase their total income, especially in regions with low unemployment or a large informal sector. As a result, a vast majority of workers – over 80 percent for men – chose or were forced into early retirement.[9]

The rapid increase in the number of pensioners was in a way a transitional phenomenon, and its impact will dissipate over time. However, the consequences of an increase in the replacement rate will have a long lasting and more serious impact on pension expenditures in the long term.

Reducing the generosity of the pension system would reduce pension costs, but politically this is not an easy option since the high replacement rate resulted from a political decision in the first place. The introduction of a generous pension formula and favorable indexation of pensions have both been motivated by strong political and moral pressures to improve the welfare of pensioners.[10] It is similarly difficult to withdraw provisions allowing higher benefits and early retirement for many occupational groups (e.g., miners, railroad workers, teachers, and police).

Although the transition has imposed considerable financial stress on pension systems across the region, the situation in Poland stands out as the most dramatic in terms of costs.[11] Poland has one of the most expensive pension systems in the region despite also having the most favorable demographic situation (the lowest old-age dependency ratio). At the same time, it has a relatively high system dependency ratio[12] and one of the highest replacement rates. While most countries reduced the generosity of their pension systems to offset growth in system dependency rates, the Polish government increased the replacement rate, thus compounding the increase in costs. The replacement rate of 72 percent in Poland far exceeds that in the Czech Republic and Slovakia (45 percent) or Hungary (47 percent).

---

[9]   The median retirement age is 59 for men and 54 for women.

[10]   For example, if a worker retires after 45 years of work and his pre-retirement wage equals the average wage in the economy, then he receives a pension equal to 83 percent of previous earnings, indexed to wage growth.

[11]   This paragraph draws on Andrews and Rashid (1996).

[12]   Relatively high system dependency ratios result not only from policies favoring early retirement but also from very liberal conditions for granting disability pensions. The pensions are granted on the basis of the loss of faculty rather than loss of earning capacity. In consequence, 12 percent of the population aged 18 or older receives disability pensions and 37 percent of all pensioners are for disability.

Summary

- Contrary to expectations and conventional knowledge, the economic transition in Poland has not led to diminishing the welfare state built during the communist period. Indeed, the welfare state has grown even bigger. Social expenditures now account for a much larger share of the GDP than before the transition. Spending on cash transfers, especially pensions, has risen considerably not only relative to GDP but also in real terms, despite an initial steep fall in the national income. However, spending on social services such as health care and education, while remaining roughly stable as a share of GDP, has suffered from the recession and has fallen in real terms.

- Social spending is extremely high in Poland, given a relatively low GDP level and large development needs. Moreover, during the transition public resources were shifted from expenditures in kind, such as education and health care, to expenditures in cash, such as pensions and social assistance. Thus, exorbitant social transfers consumed resources that could otherwise have been used for investment and thus are likely to impede economic growth. Reforming the social protection system to enhance its efficiency is a matter of the highest priority. Successful reform should free resources for investment, including investment in human capital to raise productivity and improve prospects for growth.

- Spending on pensions is the single largest component of social expenditure. Poland has one of the most costly public pension systems in Central and Eastern Europe. These high pension costs do not result from an unfavorable demographic situation but from a generous system and plentiful opportunities for early retirement. Lax eligibility for disability pensions has added to financial stress. This points to the direction and major objectives of reform: to reduce the generosity of the public pension system, to create disincentives for early retirement, and to restrict the eligibility for early retirement and disability pensions.

- Contrary to early expectations, the costs of unemployment and poverty in the wake of economic restructuring have not been the major factor behind the rise in social expenditures. Rather, the problem has been the skyrocketing costs of the pension system. This remains true even after taking into account that some pensions were substituted for unemployment benefits through early safety net programs. The increase in cash transfers has been far greater than that required by the emergence of unemployment and a related lack of incomes.

- Extensive expectations that the state should meet social needs, coupled with the democratic process, have led to the rapid growth of the welfare state during the transition. The natural reaction of the fledging democracy has been to respond to voters' needs and expectations. Now Poland faces, in an acute form, many of the problems with welfare state reform that plague developed Western countries. In contrast to early assumptions about the declining role of the state during the transition, the welfare state in Poland has grown to its limits and curtailing it has become a major challenge for the next phase of reforms.

2

Changes In The Labor Market: Emerging Risks And Opportunities

Introduction: the emergence of labor markets

A competitive labor market has emerged in the wake of transition, including open unemployment and changes in the mechanism for setting wages. Under central planning the risk of unemployment was virtually nonexistent. This is no longer the case. Once they became exposed to internal and external competition and facing hard budget constraints, firms began to shed redundant labor. Unemployment in Poland grew rapidly, peaking at 16 percent of the labor force in the early years of transition before declining to 12 percent in the late 1990s. Joblessness has hit some groups of workers more than others. Some unemployed workers have been quite successful in finding new jobs, while others have remained unemployed for a long time, and still others have become discouraged by the difficulties of finding a job and have withdrawn from the labor force.

Development of the private sector, decentralization of wage setting, and various demand shifts have caused the wage structure to move toward a new equilibrium. Relative wages have changed, meaning gains for some worker groups and loses for others. Wage dispersion has increased as opportunities for high earnings have emerged, but simultaneously more workers have found themselves at the bottom of earnings distribution.

Changes in the labor market have entailed the transition from a world of jobs that were equally good (or equally bad) to jobs that differ considerably in terms of job security and reward. Which worker groups have seen improved opportunities for good jobs and which have seen increased risks of low pay or unemployment? Do active labor market programs improve the chances of workers with least competitive capacity? It is useful to couch these questions in terms of human capital theory. Has the transition brought about an increase in returns to human capital, which were traditionally low under central planning? What are the human capital characteristics conducive to good employment and earnings prospects? Are labor market programs targeted at those with a low level of human capital?

The transition in Poland caused a remarkable increase in returns to labor market skills and education that has been the major factor behind the rise in wage dispersion. This process has been spearheaded by the private sector, where educational premia and wage dispersion have been considerably higher than in the public sector. High skills have also become the best protection against unemployment, while low skills often lead to joblessness. Active labor market programs do not significantly improve the long-term prospects of those who are most disadvantaged on the labor market – the poorly educated workers.

Employment opportunities and the risk of unemployment

Differences in educational attainment translate into unequal job opportunities. Well-educated workers face a low risk of unemployment and if they do become unemployed, they tend to find new jobs relatively quickly. In contrast, workers with lower skills often find themselves without jobs and have difficulty finding more work. Insufficient skills account for a non-negligible part of Polish unemployment and active labor-market programs hardly improve the prospects of low-skilled workers. Training courses, which are by far the most successful in bringing the unemployed back to work, are largely given to more skilled workers and thus make the initial differences in job chances even larger. Subsidized employment programs are targeted at the disadvantaged on the labor market but their scale and impact are limited.

Education, skills and unemployment. The better the educational attainment the lower the risk of unemployment (Figure 2.1). In this respect the Polish labor market resembles that in developed-market economies. The unemployment rate among university graduates is 3 percent, whereas among workers with less than secondary education it is around 15 percent.

Figure 2.1   Unemployment rates by educational attainment, 1995

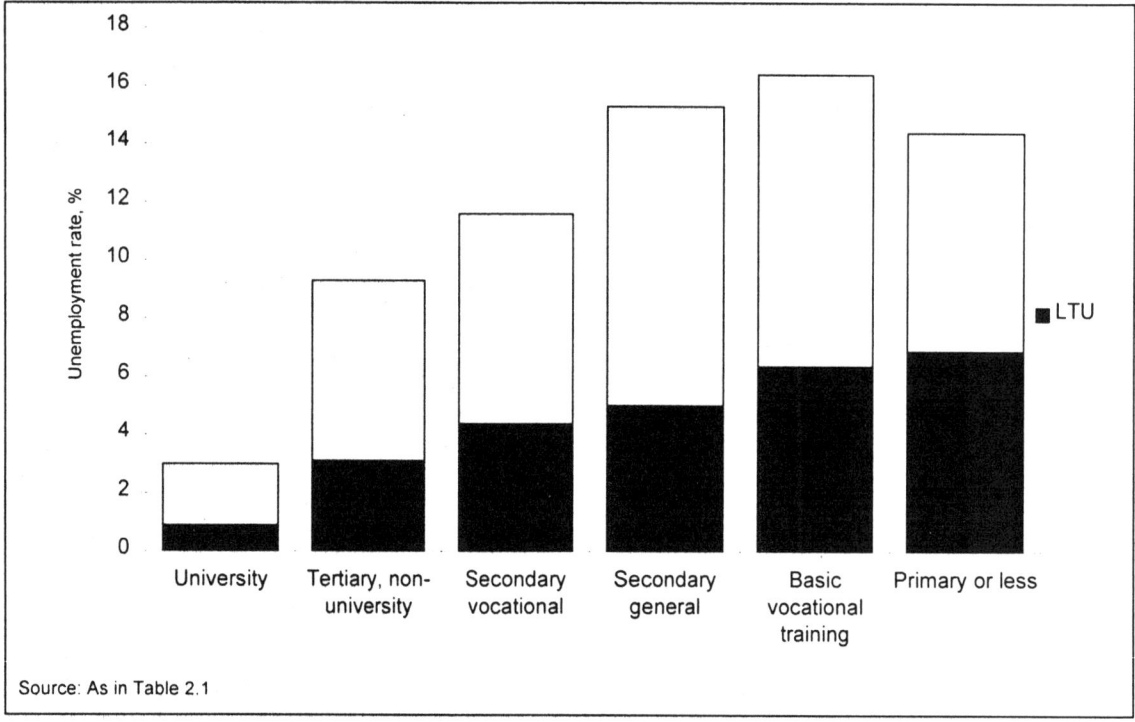

Source: As in Table 2.1

For workers with basic vocational training (the most common form of vocational education in Poland), the risk of unemployment is five times as high as for a university-educated worker and 1.5 times higher than for a worker with secondary technical education.[14] The risk of unemployment is also substantial for high school graduates, who have an unemployment rate of 15 percent. The best protection against unemployment is a university education and, to a lesser degree, secondary technical education, while lack of skills or narrow vocational skills substantially increase the risk of joblessness.

High unemployment rates among workers with basic vocational training can be explained by overspecialization, i.e., having narrow and non-transferable skills, and, more generally, by the decline in demand for less-skilled, blue-collar labor.[15]

In recent years, the world has experienced what is referred to as "non-neutral technical progress," that is, technical change biased in favor of more skilled workers. There is no reason to think that Poland is exempt from this process. The opening of the economy in the wake of market- oriented reforms, the increase in foreign trade, and the inflow of direct foreign investment have all brought in new technology. Economic restructuring, consisting of the shift from overdeveloped manufacturing and heavy industry to the service sector, including expanding sectors such as banking, finance, and business services, has reinforced this trend. Service-sector workers are often required to use modern office technology and be computer-literate, skills that manual workers typically lack. Given the current labor supply, employers can substitute workers with technical secondary education for workers with basic vocational training and workers with a college degree for workers with secondary general education. Employers will do this as long as the productivity differential is greater than wage differential. This points to the importance of wage adjustment, which will be discussed later.

Less-educated workers, who face a high risk of unemployment, often tend to withdraw from the labor force. Conversely, highly educated workers, who are rarely unemployed, have high labor force participation rates (Table 2.1). For example, the labor force participation rate for college- educated workers is 5 percentage points higher than for workers with basic vocational training. This may provide some indirect evidence of the discouraged worker effect, whereby workers withdraw from the labor force because their job search efforts have proved futile. Higher labor force participation, coupled with lower unemployment, is likely to contribute to higher incomes for families with more human capital.

Long-term unemployment can be socially dangerous. It is associated with erosion of skills and morale and a low probability of re-employment. Because employers view long-term unemployment as a signal of low productivity, it can eventually lead to social marginalization and poverty.

---

[14]   However, informal sector employment somewhat mitigates these disparities. About 11 percent of all workers with basic vocational training have a job in the informal sector, compared with 5 and 7 percent of workers with secondary or higher education. For over 40 percent of workers with basic vocational education, informal sector jobs are the main source of income. This is less often the case for better educated workers (Kalaska and Witkowski 1995).

[15]   The steady collapse in the demand for low-skilled labor is sometimes considered "[...] perhaps the greatest single problem confronting modern industrial societies," (Layard 1996).

The risk is highest for poorly educated workers. For example, the incidence of long-term unemployment among workers with basic vocational training (40 percent) is greater than among workers with a university diploma (30 percent). The average duration of job search is shorter for better-educated workers. On average, university-educated workers look for a job for four months less than workers with basic vocational training and three months less than workers with general secondary education. Similarly, exit rates from unemployment strongly depend on educational attainment. The exit rate for university-educated workers is twice as high as for workers with basic vocational training and three times as high as for workers with primary education. All these examples reinforce the point that low skills mean bad labor market prospects and can lead to prolonged unemployment.

However, employment prospects are influenced by factors other than education. Age, gender, and place of residence also affect unemployment, job search duration, and the chances of finding a job. But as Table 2.1 documents, their role is minor in comparison with that of education. Education is the single most important factor determining labor market prospects and points to the role of skill mismatch in generating unemployment.

To assess the importance of the skill mismatch, imagine that the number of available jobs grows to the point where there are enough jobs for everyone who is unemployed. Assume that jobs for each educational category grow at the same rate. In such a best-case scenario, where the number of vacancies equals the number of job seekers, about 14 percent of all unemployed will not find a job because of skill mismatch, that is, because their skills do not meet employers' requirements. Given the current unemployment rate of about 14 percent, this implies a 2 percent unemployment rate caused by skill mismatch.[16] As might be expected, the problem of skill mismatch is more severe among the long-term unemployed. In this case inadequate skills prevent 17 percent of the long-term unemployed from finding work, despite the general availability of jobs. The skill mismatch is most pronounced among those with only basic vocational training. They constitute some 45 percent of all unemployed, while jobs requiring basic vocational training account for only one-third of all jobs.

A partial solution to the problem of skill mismatch is to increase workforce skill levels through general education and training . But in the face of falling demand for low-skilled labor, the problem of low-skilled workers, for whom the costs of learning new skills are high, will remain. Better education and better training may not be sufficiently effective in the case of slow learners. In such cases the only solution may be greater wage flexibility, allowing low-ability workers to price themselves into the job market. At the macro level, this would imply trading off more earnings dispersion for more equitable access to jobs.

---

[16] This is a lower bound estimate of the magnitude of the skill mismatch because of the best-case scenario assumption. The actual magnitude of the skill mismatch problem is probably much larger, given that skill mismatches are also likely to occur within educational categories and the labor demand is likely to grow more in the more education/skill intensive jobs.

Table 2.1 Labor market prospects by age, gender education and place of residence, 1995

	Labor force participation rate	Unemployment rate	Incidence of long-term unemployment
		In percent	
Gender			
Men	66,5	12,1	35,6
Women	51,1	14,4	44,2
Age			
15-17	3,7	15,6	16,6
18-19	36,6	48,4	
20-24	68,3	27,1	33,8
25-29	82,9	14,5	38,7
30-34	87,3	13,4	41,3
35-39	88,6	11,4	46,2
40-44	86,5	10,1	
45-49	81,6	8,4	51,6
50-54	68,3	8,0	
55-59	42,0	7,2	
60-64	25,0	4,0	50,0
65+	10,3	1,8	
Educational attainment			
All levels	58,4	13,1	39,9
University	81,3	3,0	30,2
Tertiary, non-university	83,4	9,3	33,3
Secondary vocational	74,5	11,6	37,7
Secondary general	50,1	15,3	32,7
Basic vocational training	76,5	16,4	38,8
Primary or less	33,2	14,4	47,8
Place of residence			
Urban	57,2	13,7	40,4
More than 500 thosand inhabitants	54,9	9,0	-
100 - 500 thousand	56,2	13,6	-
50 - 100 thousand	58,0	15,7	-
20 - 50 thousand	58,8	15,1	-
10 - 20 thousand	59,2	15,7	-
Less than 10 thousand	58,9	16,9	-
Rural	60,5	12,2	38,9

- Data not available

Source: Aktywnosc Ekonomiczna Ludnosci Polski: Maj 1995, GUS, Warszawa; author's calculations

Policy response to unemployment. Labor markets generate considerable inequality in access to jobs. Education and skills are the major dimension of this inequality. What has been the policy response to inequality of employment opportunities? Is it driven by equity or efficiency considerations?[17] Do active labor market policies improve the chances of participants to find employment, and thus reduce inequality in access to jobs?

There are three major types of active labor market policies (ALMPs) in Poland: labor market training, wage subsidies, referred to as "intervention works," and direct job creation, referred to as "public works." The scope of these programs is limited. The most popular are wage subsidies which are granted to about 6 percent of the unemployed. Public works participants account for nearly 5 percent of all unemployed, and enrollment in training courses is close to 4 percent (GUS, 1997).

Is targeting of active labor market programs equitable? Subsidized employment programs, both wage subsidies and public works, are targeted at less skilled workers. About three quarters of the participants of these programs have less than secondary education. Given that poorly educated workers face the highest risk of unemployment, targeting of subsidized employment programs is carried out on equity grounds.

Training courses, by contrast, are primarily offered to workers with a university degree, somewhat less frequently to workers with high school education and seldom to workers without secondary education.[18] Given that well educated workers face a relatively low risk of unemployment, selection for training is not done on equity grounds. Rather, it is cost-effectiveness that drives training offers, since targeting training at those unemployed with relatively high re-employment probabilities results in the lowest cost per job placement. Thus, it is hardly surprising that training is found to be the most cost-effective active labor measure in Poland. High cost-effectiveness largely reflects the selection process whereby training tends to be received by the unemployed who have the best chances of finding a job anyway.

Targeting training to better educated workers is not only the result of the decisions made by the staff of employment offices, but also a result of the preferences of the unemployed. Willingness to participate in training courses is directly related to educational attainment. Gora et al. (1995) report that more than half of the unemployed without secondary education do not want to become enrolled in training, even if its publicly financed.

---

[17]   Efficiency considerations prevail if labor market programs are targeted at those unemployed who benefit (in terms of the gain in re-employment probability) the most. On the other hand, equity reasons prevail if policies are targeted at those unemployed with least competitive capacity and correspondingly low employment probabilities. There may be a trade-off: focusing on the most difficult cases implies high costs, which are accompanied by comparatively low effects in terms of job placement. On the other hand, "cream skimming" implies that those with the least competitive capacity are left out.

[18]   Training courses are offered to 10 percent of unemployed university educated workers, 8 percent of high school educated workers and 4 percent of the unemployed without secondary education (Gora et al. 1995).

In contrast, one-fifth of the unemployed with a university degree would like to participate in training, even if they had to pay the costs. As a result, actual participation in training courses is even more differentiated by education than the training offers. Training is received by almost 8 percent of unemployed with a university degree, 5 percent of unemployed with secondary education and less than 2 percent unemployed without secondary education.

As a result, training increases rather than decreases inequality in employment chances by increasing initial human capital differentials. In this respect Poland is not different from other countries, since it is an empirical regularity that training participation is correlated with education. Nevertheless, the point remains valid that existing training programs do not address the problem of low skills.

Is targeting of active labor programs allocatively efficient? That is, are programs targeted at groups that benefit most from them? In order to answer this question satisfactorily one must gauge the gain in re-employment probability from program participation for different groups of the unemployed, for example for the well educated and poorly educated. Unfortunately, information on the differences in re-employment probabilities between similar workers (i.e. workers of similar age, educational attainment, etc.) who did and did not participate in a program is not available. Thus, a rigorous answer is not possible at the moment.[19] Puhani and Steiner (1996) provide an approximate answer based on an assessment of the impact of program participation done by the unemployed themselves.

Subsidized employment programs (intervention and public works) are judged especially helpful by the unemployed without much labor market experience – especially young people – and by the unemployed without specific vocational skills (i.e. with primary or secondary general education). However, they are gauged not to be useful by workers performing simple manual jobs. These results are puzzling, as one would be inclined to assume that low education and simple jobs go hand in hand. Evidence on allocative efficiency is, in this case, mixed and somewhat ambiguous. Targeting of employment subsidies is efficient to the extent that participants are poorly educated workers. However, it is not efficient if the participants are laborers and other workers doing simple jobs.

Training seems to benefit the unemployed with less than secondary education the most. In this case, the gain in re-employment probability from the training participation accounts for 10 percent, compared to the mere 3-4 percent for the unemployed with secondary or higher education (Gora et al., 1995).[20] This suggests that targeting of training programs is not allocatively efficient. Those who benefit most from training – the less educated – are the minority among training participants.

---

[19]   A specially designed study of the net impact of active labor programs in Poland is under way. The study will make it possible to evaluate the efficiency of the programs more rigorously.

[20]   These results are not adjusted for the possible selection bias.

This supports the earlier finding that the current approach to training of the unemployed seems to be driven mainly by cost-effectiveness (low cost per placement), and less by efficiency, measured by the gain in re-employment probability per unit of cost. This "cream skimming" results in high job insertion rates for ex-trainees, however it is usually associated with heavy dead-weight loss, that is government paying for the outcome that would have happened anyway. If so, then training programs which are presently run in Poland do not seem to be the most efficient use of public resources.

To summarize, targeting of marginal employment subsidies seems both equitable and – at least to some degree – allocatively efficient. That is, the subsidies are targeted at groups that are the most disadvantaged on the labor market, and simultaneously benefit the most from program participation. In contrast, targeting of training programs is rarely done on equity grounds, and the available evidence suggests that it is not allocatively efficient. Training tends to be received by groups with relatively high competitive capacity and thus exacerbates inequalities in employment chances. At the same time, training is hardly received by those who seem to get the most out of it, that is by the less educated.

A more general question regards the impact of active labor market policies on employment. Do ALMPs reduce unemployment? Do they improve employment prospects of participants? The existing evidence – which is scant and tentative – on the macroeconomic and microeconomic effects of ALMPs in Poland is not encouraging. The results of a macro-econometric impact analysis done for Poland using 1994 data show "no significant effect of ALMP expenditure on the outflow rate from unemployment into employment" (Puhani and Steiner, 1996). In other words, the ALMPs in Poland seem not to have a discernible impact on the level of unemployment.

Even if their direct macroeconomic impact is insignificant, ALMPs still can play a useful role if they redistribute job opportunities toward the groups disadvantaged in the labor market, such as the long-term unemployed, low skilled, etc.. In this case ALMPs reduce the risk that these disadvantaged groups leave the labor force, and thus help maintaining the effective supply of labor. This means that there will be more competition for available jobs, which should reduce wage pressure, and eventually, raise employment.

Available evidence suggests that the impact of ALMPs on employment prospects of participants is at best moderate, although it differs by program. The re-employment rate for public works, which are intended as a bridge to regular employment, is less than 8 percent. Only half of participants of intervention works keep their job after the one year. In the case of training the success (job accession) rate looks more promising, as close to 60 percent of ex-trainees find a job one year after program completion. However, a high success rate by itself is not very informative as long as it is not possible to compare it with the job accession rate of the unemployed with similar characteristics who did not participate in a program. The crude job accession rate tends to overestimate the actual impact of a program participation, since it does not control for the selection bias, that is the fact that program participants tend to differ from non-participants in that they have personal attributes conducive to employment.

The unemployed themselves do not deem job insertion programs as particularly helpful, either. As much as 80 percent of participants of subsidized employment programs view them as useless in terms of improving their employment prospects (Kostrubiec and Kowalska, 1997). Training scores better on the subjective assessment scale, although still one-third of ex-trainees consider its impact as negligible, and only one-fourth as highly significant.

The lack of a clear success of ALMPs in combating unemployment is not specific to Poland. Employment promotion policies, in general, work on the margin. Unemployment is not a result of the lack of adequate labor market policies. Rather, it stems from macroeconomic policies, aggregate demand conditions, product market competitiveness, labor market institutions and flexibility. Correspondingly, labor market polices are not a solution to unemployment. Their role is to lessen the hardship associated with unemployment, and to help those who are disadvantaged on the labor market and can benefit from temporary interventions. In many cases labor market policies merely redistribute employment opportunities, rather than create truly new jobs. The prevailing evidence shows that their net effect is relatively small (OECD, 1993).

To sum up, the tentative evidence suggests the labor market policies that have been carried out in Poland have not significantly enhanced equality in access to jobs. They cover a small fraction of the unemployed, and are at best moderately effective in improving their employment prospects. Subsidized employment programs are targeted at the most disadvantaged and by and large at those who benefit most from them. However, their overall success rate is rather low. In contrast, training courses are attended largely by the better educated unemployed who are in an advantageous position in the labor market, and who are likely to find a job anyway. If so, training programs in Poland do not lead to a substantial improvement in employment prospects, notwithstanding their high success rate. Although the most cost effective among ALMPs, training programs neither have a substantial net impact, nor equalize employment prospects.

The following policy recommendations grow out of these findings. A better use of public resources requires collecting information as to the costs and benefits of ALMPs. Currently such information is incomplete, and thus it is uncertain to what degree different labor market programs improve employment prospects of program participants. To address this problem, the assessment of the net impact of ALMPs should be carried out to determine what is the efficacy of different programs and which groups of the unemployed benefit most from each program. Given this information, resources should be re-allocated towards the programs that are found to have the largest net impact. Within each program participants should be selected so as to meet, to the extent possible, simultaneously, equity and efficiency objective. This implies targeting participants who belong to groups disadvantaged in the labor market (such as the less educated and less skilled) and, at the same time, who are likely to benefit most from program participation. Special carefully designed and small scale programs should be developed to address well identified needs of problem groups among the unemployed, including the most difficult cases (such as persons abusing alcohol, ex-prisoners, etc.) These measures, if implemented, will assure more efficient use of public resources even if the impact of ALMPs on the aggregate unemployment to employment will remain limited.

Changes in the wage structure

Unemployment is one source of inequality generated by the labor market. The other is wage dispersion. Economic liberalization has brought about a substantial increase in wage dispersion in Poland, a process that occurred in all transitional economies. This rise in wage dispersion has been driven largely by rising returns to education. The private sector has led the changes; inequalities there are substantially greater compared to the public sector, and so are the returns to education. This section addressees in more detail the issues of wage differentials, wage developments in the private sector, and returns to education.

Rising wage differentials. Earnings distribution has widened considerably in Poland during the transition (Figure 2.2). The Gini coefficient – a summary measure of inequality – reached 29 in 1995, up from 21-23 in the late 1980s. This is a significant, though not dramatic, rise. Low- paid workers have lost ground relative to the median, that is, the earnings "poverty gap" has increased, although modestly. Presently a worker in the bottom decile earns 42 percent less than the median worker, while in the late 1980s the gap was 35-39 percent. However, the most dramatic change has taken place at the top of the scale. A worker in the top decile earns twice as much as the median worker, whereas before the transition he earned only 1.6 times as much. As a result, the earnings differential between the lowest and highest-paid workers has increased considerably. A high- paid worker now earns 3.4 times as much as a low-paid worker, up from 2.4-2.8 times before the transition.

The practical meaning of rising wage differentials is that some workers gain relative to others, while some lose. However, if the average wage does not rise then the relative loss implies also an absolute loss. This is the case in Poland, where the average wage has not yet fully recovered from a sharp drop at the outset of transition. About one-half of workers still receive real wages lower than before the transition (Figure 2.3). The biggest losers are those in the bottom decile, while the biggest gainers are those in the top decile. Although the fraction of those who suffered a fall in real wages is large, the consoling fact is that the loss they have experienced is small, unlike some other transition economies, and can be made up relatively quickly if output continues to grow.

Figure 2.2   Changes in earnings distribution, 1987-1995

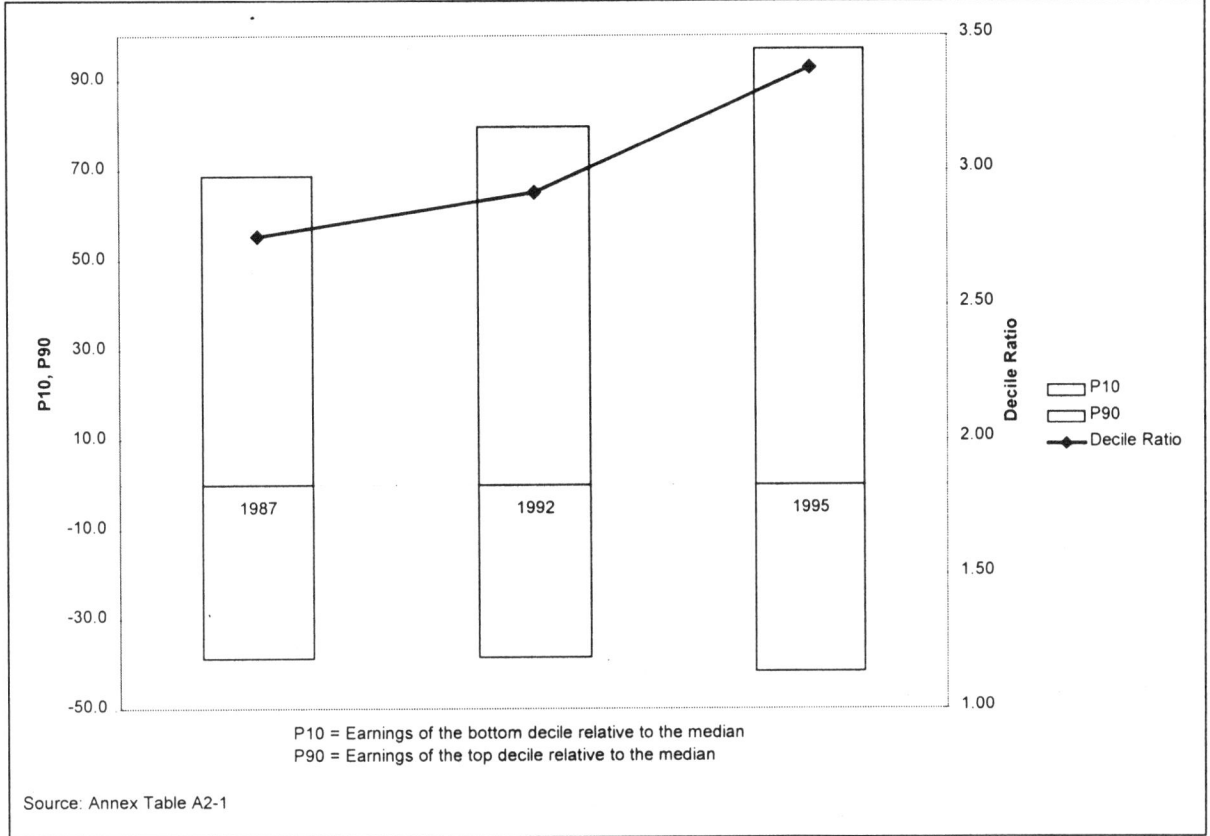

P10 = Earnings of the bottom decile relative to the median
P90 = Earnings of the top decile relative to the median

Source: Annex Table A2-1

The change in wage distribution in Poland is similar to that in virtually all transitional economies in Central and Eastern Europe (Rutkowski, 1996b). The increase in wage inequality and the level of inequality is comparable to that of other CEE countries (Figure 2.4, Panel A). For example, wage inequality in Poland is similar to that observed in, the Czech Republic, and Slovenia, although it is significantly lower than in Hungary (by 4 Gini points). The only CEE country with significantly lower earnings inequality than in Poland is Slovak Republic, which has preserved the wage distribution inherited from the past.

The earnings status of both low- and high-paid workers in Poland is somewhat better than in many CEE countries (Figure 2.4, Panels B and C). This implies that wage inequality in Poland largely springs from higher earnings at the top rather than by lower earnings at the bottom. For instance, a lowest-decile worker in Hungary earns 55 percent of the median, compared to almost 60 percent in Poland. At the same time, a highest-decile worker in the Czech Republic earns 80 percent more than the median worker, whereas his Polish counterpart earns twice as much as the median worker.

Figure 2.3   Real wage growth by selected percentiles (1987 =100)

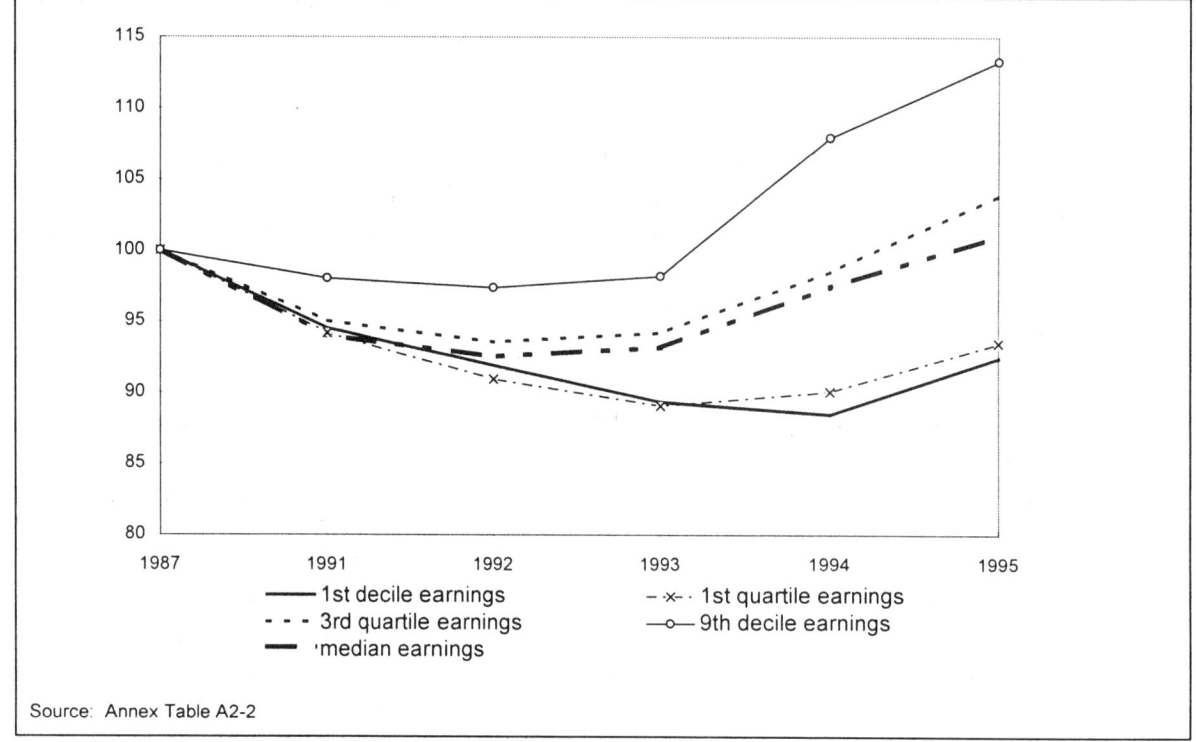

Source: Annex Table A2-2

At present the level of wage inequality in Poland is at the upper end of the OECD range (Figure 2.5). This is a big change, for before transition wage inequality in Poland (as in other centrally planned economies) was low compared to market economies. Although the decile ratio[21] of 3.4 observed in Poland is high by European standards, it is quite modest by world standards. For instance, in the US the decile ratio is as high as 5.6. It is noteworthy that earnings inequality in Poland is greater than in such countries as France, where the decile ratio amounts to 3.0, Portugal (2.6), Germany (2.5), or Italy (2.1) and similar to that prevailing in Austria or the UK (OECD 1993).

Rising wage dispersion causes increased incidence of both low and high pay. However, the increase in the incidence of low pay that has occurred in Poland during the transition has not been great.[22] Now low-paid workers account for 17 percent of all workers, up from 14 percent in 1987.[23] In the Czech Republic or Slovenia the rise in the number of low-paid workers was considerably greater and their number is higher than in Poland (Figure 2.6). The percentage of low-paid workers in Poland is somewhat higher than in the majority

---

[21]   The decile ratio is the ratio of top decile earnings to bottom decile earnings.

[22]   Low pay is defined as earnings lower than two-thirds of the median earnings.

[23]   The data refer to the formal sector only, which may bias the results. According to anecdotal evidence, earnings in the informal sector are on average significantly lower than in the formal sector. However, insofar as "low pay" is defined relative to median earnings, the direction of the bias is ambiguous, since the inclusion of the informal sector would also shift the median. Thus, it is not possible assert *a priori* that the inclusion of the informal sector would result in an increase in the incidence of low pay.

of European OECD countries (Figure 2.7). For example, it is higher than in France or Germany, close to that in Ireland, but is substantially lower than in the United Kingdom or the United States.

The increase in the incidence of low pay has contributed to the growth in the number of "working poor," who account for 60 percent of the total poor (World Bank, 1995).[24] This increase in poverty is the most socially adverse manifestation of greater wage inequality. Fortunately, neither the increase in the incidence of low pay nor deterioration of the earnings position of low-paid workers has been very strong in Poland, so that the impact on poverty of wider earnings distribution has been limited.

With regard to the incidence of high pay, the percentage of workers receiving high wages (higher than 1.5 times the median wage) has risen quite substantially, reaching one-fifth of all workers. This means that compared to the pre-transition period, about 5 percent of workers improved their relative earnings status in that they moved from middle-ranking jobs to well-paid jobs. This gives another approximation of the number of winners in transition.

The growing number of both low-paid and high-paid jobs gives rise to concerns about the "shrinking middle," or the polarization of wages. Close to 10 percent of workers have left the middle, moving either up or down the earnings ladder. But a vast majority of workers – more than 60 percent – still earn around the median wage. Middle-ranking jobs are still preponderant, and fears of polarization seem greatly exaggerated.

---

[24]   The working poor include both working-age adults and their children.

Figure 2.4   Earnings distribution in CEE countries before and during transition

Panel A: Gini coefficient

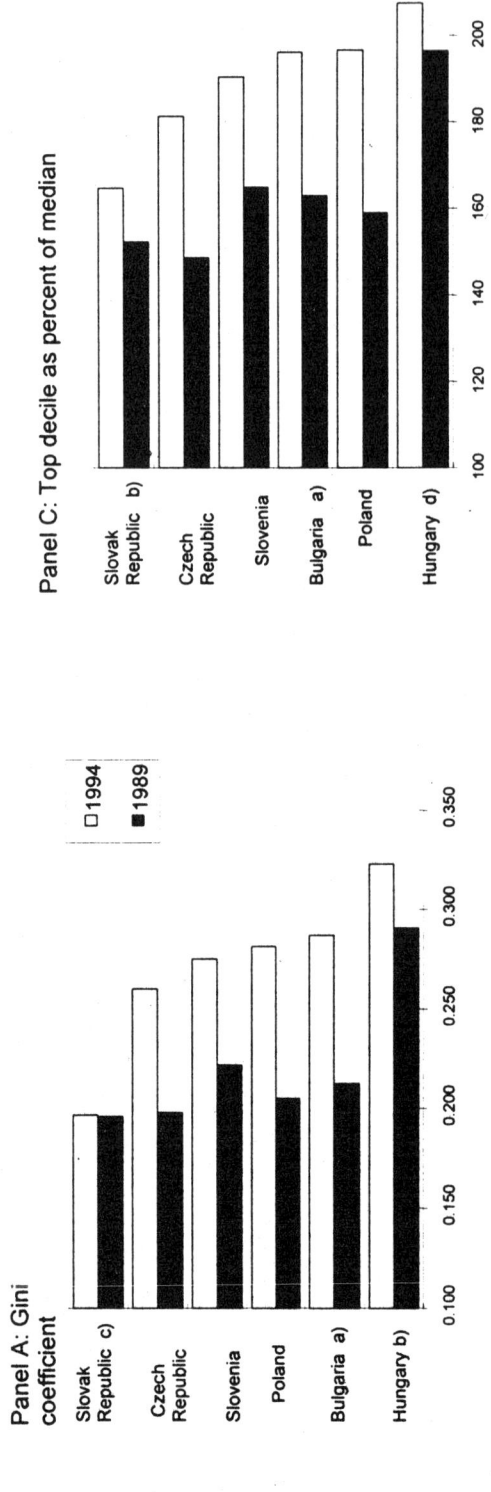

Panel B: Bottom decile as percent of median

Panel C: Top decile as percent of median

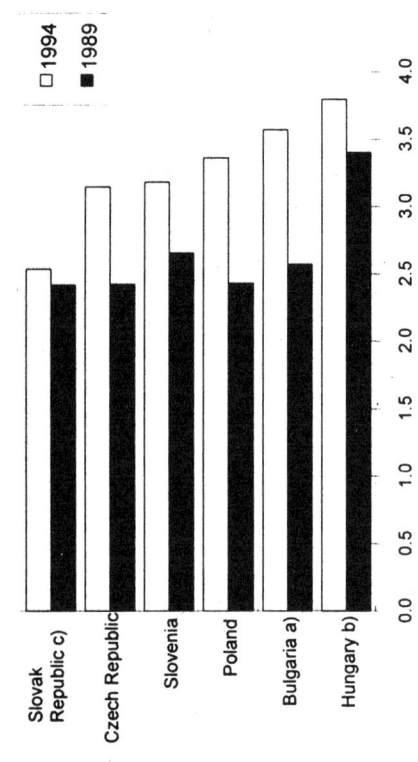

Panel D: Decile ratio

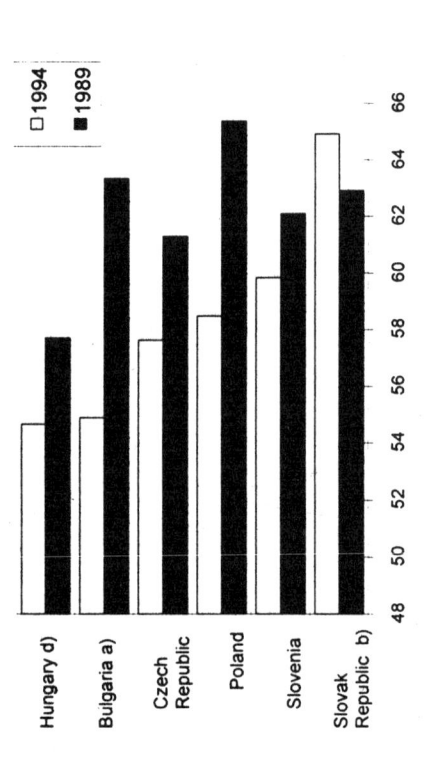

Source: Annex Table A2-3A   a) 1995 & 1990 data, b) 1990 data, c) 1993 data

Figure 2.5   Decile ratio in Poland and in selected OECD countries
(late 1980s/early 1990s)

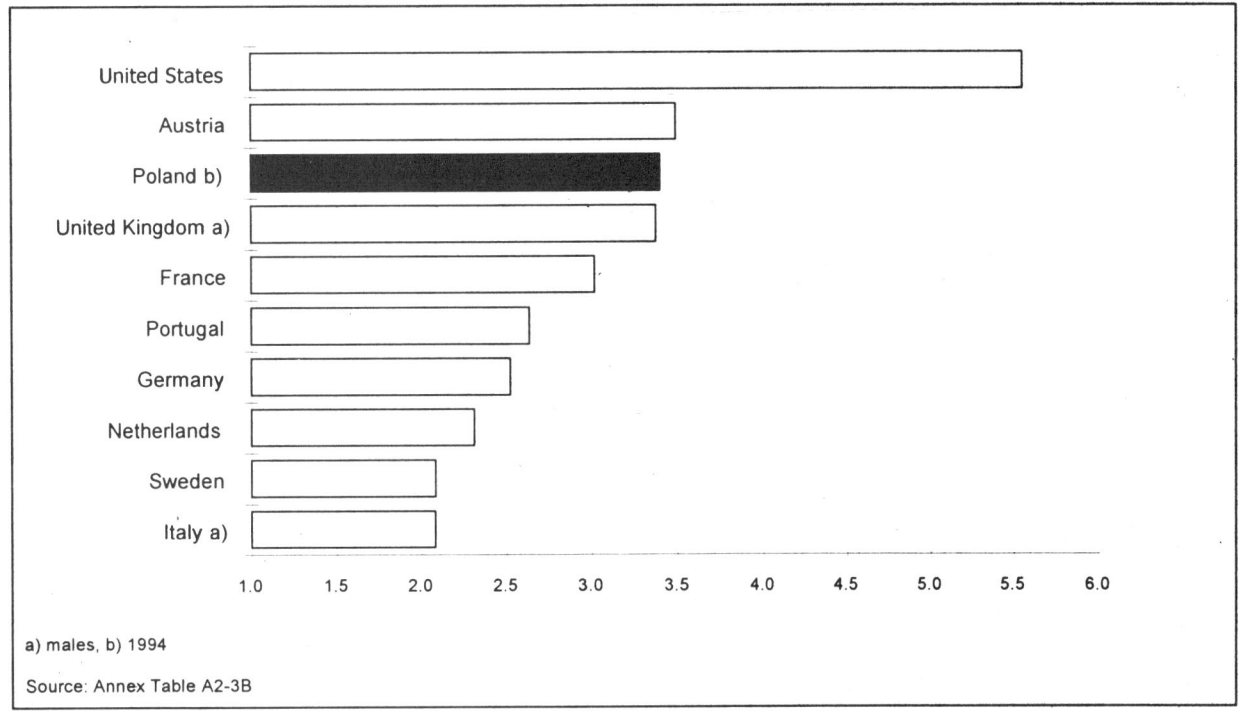

a) males, b) 1994

Source: Annex Table A2-3B

Figure 2.6   Incidence of low pay in CEE countries before and during transition

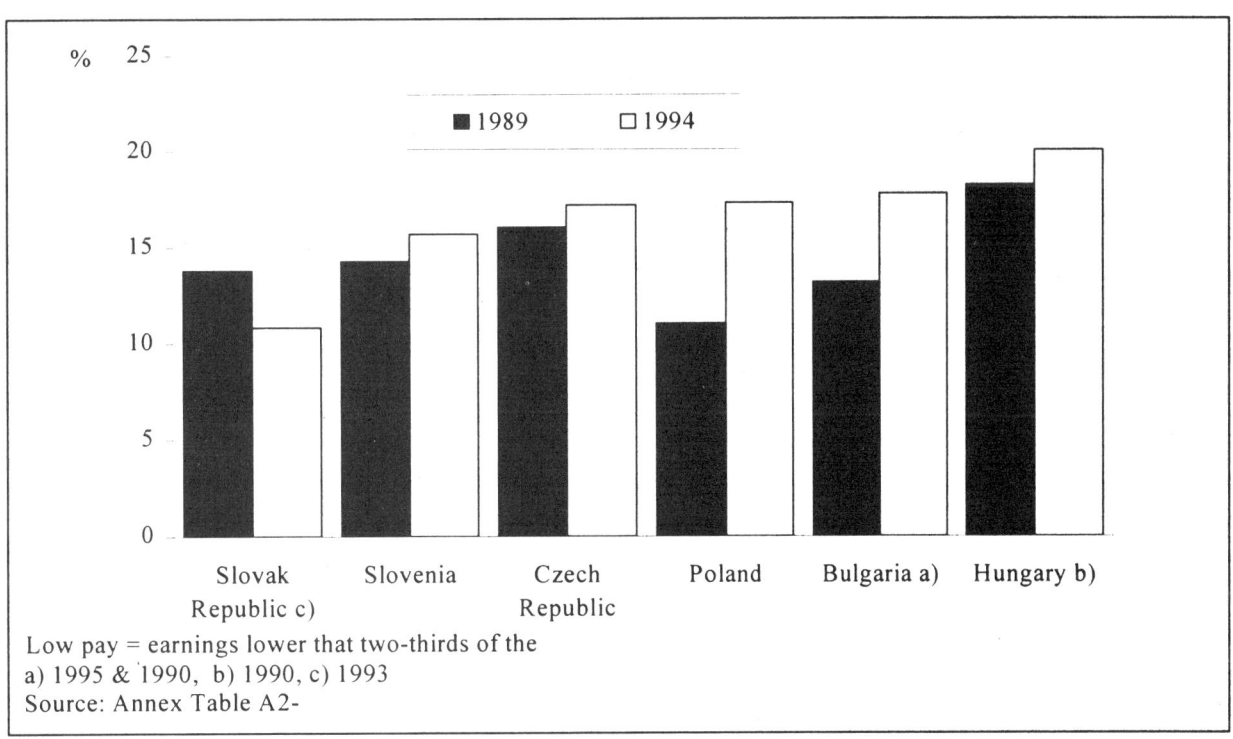

Low pay = earnings lower that two-thirds of the
a) 1995 & 1990, b) 1990, c) 1993
Source: Annex Table A2-

**Figure 2.7   Incidence of low pay in Poland and in selected OECD countries
(late 1980s/early 1990s)**

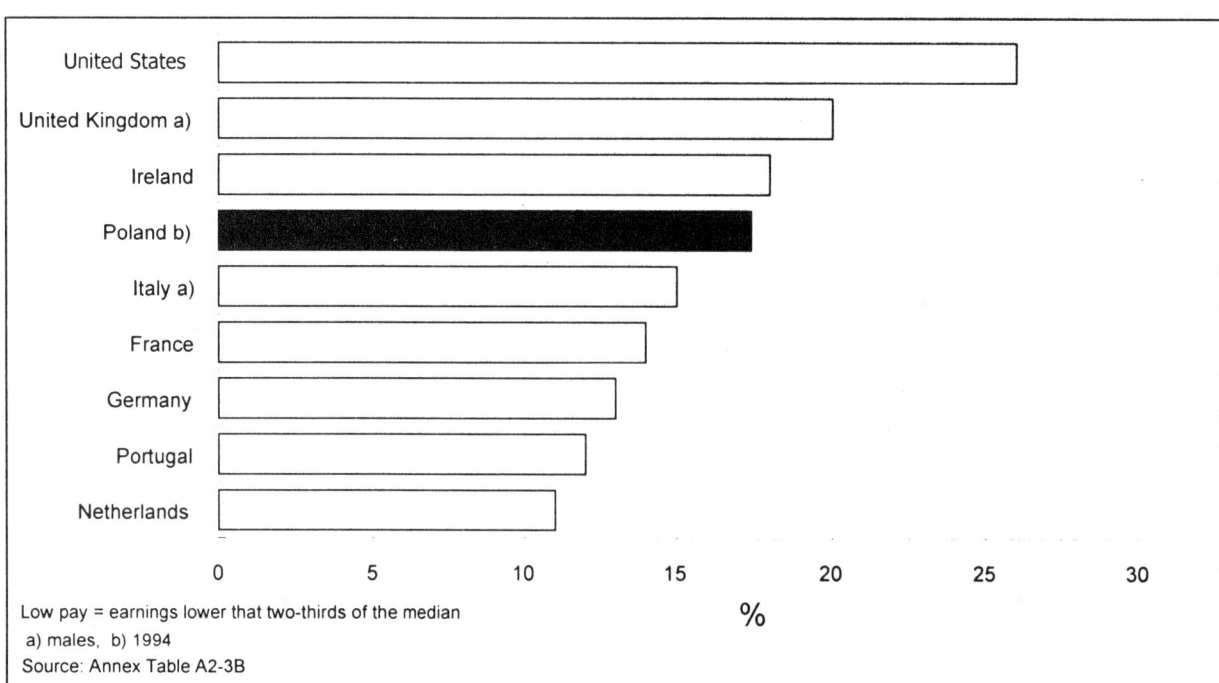

Low pay = earnings lower that two-thirds of the median
a) males, b) 1994
Source: Annex Table A2-3B

Wage developments in the private sector. Given the rising employment share of the private sector, wage developments in this sector have increasingly determined the overall wage structure. As Figure 2.8 shows, wage distribution in the private sector differs considerably from that in the public sector. The median wage in the private sector is lower than that of the public sector. Also, the majority of low-paid jobs are located in the private sector, while the public sector offers most middle to high-paying jobs. But the highest salaries are mainly found in the private sector. As a consequence, wage disparities in the private sector are visibly higher than in the public sector.

Table 2.2   gives a more detailed picture of private/public sector wage differentials. Generally, public sector employers pay their employees more than private sector employers. Private-sector workers earn on average 9 percent less than public-sector workers. [25] The private-sector pay disadvantage is especially pronounced among low-skilled workers, while it is negligible among highly skilled workers. A bottom-decile worker in the private sector earns almost one-quarter less than his public-sector counterpart. At the same time, a top-decile worker in the private sector earns only about 7 percent less than his public-sector counterpart.

---

[25]   The lower average wage in the private sector compared with the public sector may in part be a result of underreporting by the private sector for tax reasons. Moreover, the focus here is on money wages, while according to anecdotal evidence the private sector often awards workers (mainly top-paid white-collar workers) with non-wage benefits. If so, then the total emolument in the private sector may be larger than in the public sector, at least for some categories of workers.

Figure 2.8 Earnings distribution in the private and public sectors, 1995

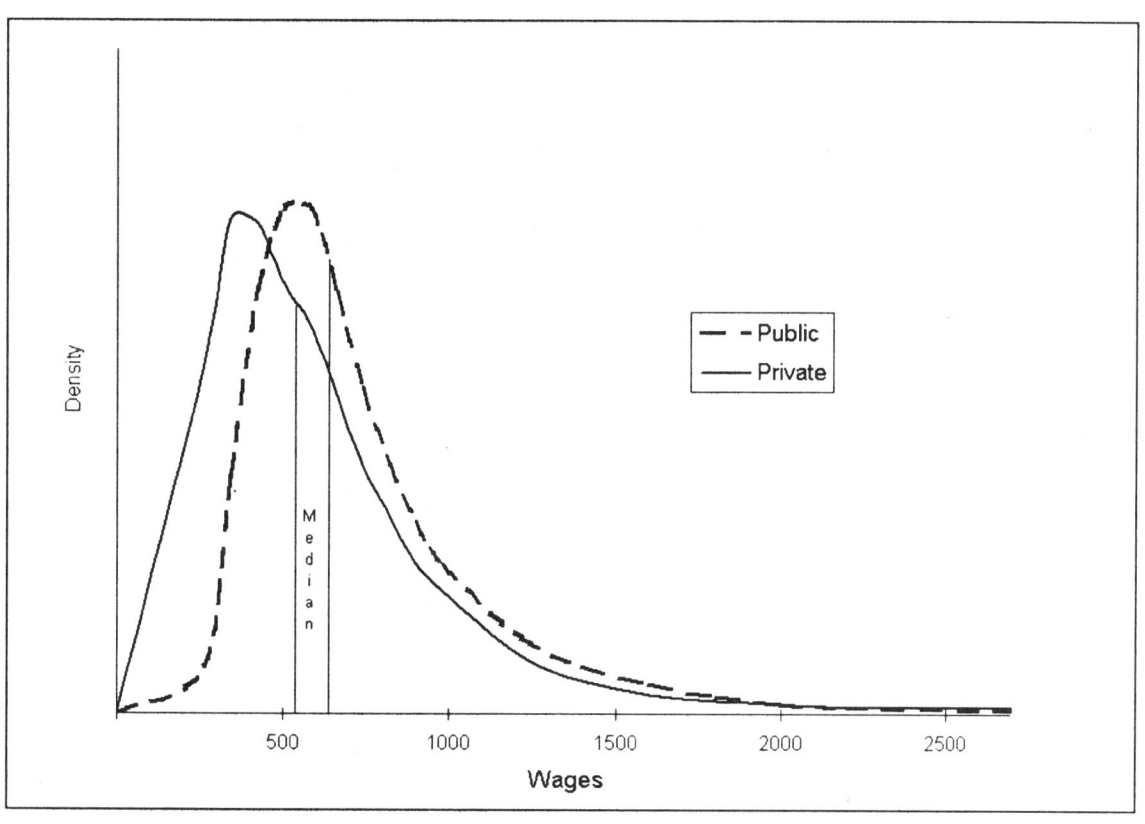

Table 2.2 Private and public sector wages by broad occupation, 1995

Wage	Private sector wage as percentage of public sector wage		
	All workers	Blue collar workers	White collar workers
Mean	91.4	81.1	117.2
Bottom decile	75.9	78.6	83.7
Median	86.9	81.8	105.5
Upper decile	92.6	77.6	129.5

Note:

Wage = net monthly earnings.

Firms employing less than 6 workers are not included in the survey.

The bottom (upper) decile wage is a wage such that 10 (90) percent of workers earn wages that are lower, and 90 (10) percent of workers earn wages that are higher.

Source: Earnings distribution as of September 1995, GUS, author's calculations.

The private/public pay differentials vary across occupational groups. Blue-collar workers are better off in the public sector, while white-collar workers are better off in the private sector. Blue-collar workers earn almost 30 percent more in the public sector than in the private sector. In contrast, the private sector offers a 17 percent pay premium to white-collar occupations.

The pay disadvantage in the private sector remains for blue-collar workers, regardless of their skills. That is, both bottom-decile and top-decile blue-collar workers lose over 20 percent in private-sector employment. In contrast, highly skilled white-collar workers gain a 30 percent premium from private-sector employment, but low-skilled white-collar workers suffer a 16 percent pay loss. Thus, the private sector rewards high white-collar skills and penalizes low white-collar and all blue-collar skills.

Wage dispersion is significantly higher in the private sector than in the public sector. In the private sector, a top-decile worker earns 3.8 times as much a bottom-decile worker. In the public sector, this decile ratio of high wages to low wages amounts to 3.1. Wage differentials in the private sector are especially large among white-collar workers, while among blue-collar workers they are substantially smaller and similar to those in the public sector. The decile ratio for white-collar private-sector workers is 4.6, compared with 3.2 for blue-collar workers in both sectors and 3.0 for white-collar public-sector workers.[26]

The private sector has turned out to be a major source of low-paying jobs, with incidence of low pay[27] strikingly higher than in the public sector (Figure 2.9, Panel A). In the private sector, low-paid jobs account for nearly 30 percent of all jobs; in the public sector it is only 12 percent. Surprisingly, the incidence of high-paid jobs[28] is also lower in the private sector (17 percent) than in the public sector (22 percent), as shown in Figure 2.9, Panel B. That is, the private sector has the highest salaries, but few people receive them. The intersectoral differences in the wage structure determine the attractiveness of both sectors for different worker groups and thus influence the mobility of workers between sectors as well as their attitude to and support of the privatization process.

Private-sector development is correctly perceived as being a cause of growing wage inequality. It is thus likely to be opposed by all those who may see their relative earnings status deteriorate. However, our analysis indicates that for many worker groups, private-sector development in the short run entails not only lower relative earnings but also, and more importantly, lower absolute earnings. This largely relates to less-skilled workers, especially blue- collar workers. There are objective premises for workers' perception that privatization endangers their earnings and jobs. In the short run, most workers often lose by moving to the private sector and thus face an incentive to stick to their public-sector jobs and oppose privatization. In contrast, highly skilled white-collar workers are the main beneficiaries of private-sector development. Thus they have a strong incentive to seek private-sector employment

---

[26]   Detailed data on wage distribution by sector are shown in Annex Table A2-4.

[27]   Low pay is defined as earnings lower than two-thirds of the median earnings in the national economy.

[28]   High pay is defined as earnings higher than 1.5 times median earnings.

and have a stake in privatization. But highly skilled white-collar workers are a minority. At the moment, the private sector does not have much to offer most workers.

Figure 2.9   Incidence of low and high pay, 1995

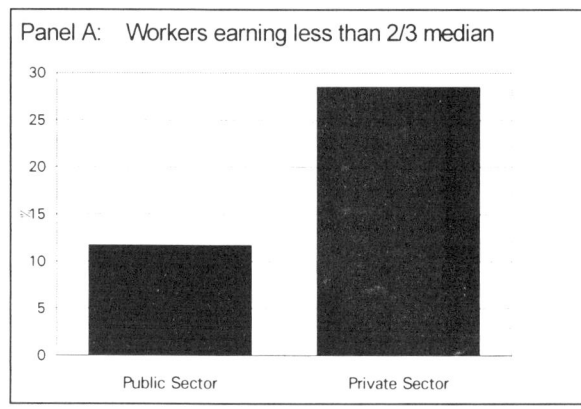
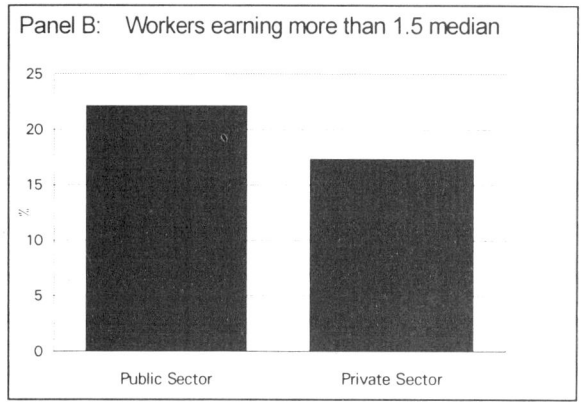

Note: Median refers to the median wage in the national economy.

Source: Annex Table A2-5

Changing returns to labor market skills. Educational premia, especially the premium to university education, have markedly increased during the transition in Poland. Table 2.3 and Figure 2.10 document this process. A university-educated worker now earns on average 50 percent more than a worker with basic vocational training. Under central planning this premium was less than 20 percent. The returns to secondary education relative to basic vocational training have also increased substantially. Before the market reforms they were actually negative: High school graduates earned less than workers with basic vocational training. Now high school graduates earn some 10 percent more than those with only basic vocational training. Tertiary education below the university level (colleges offering 1-2 year vocational courses) does not offer a significant premium. These who completed vocational colleges tend to earn less than high-school educated workers and about the same as workers with basic vocational training.

About one-third of the variance in earnings in Poland can be explained by standard human capital factors such as education, age, and gender, plus industry and sector affiliation.[29] Out of this, differences in educational attainment accounts for 12 percent of the total variance and for 35 percent of the explained variance. This is more than any other factor, such as gender (21 percent) or industry (26 percent). This impact of differences in educational attainment on wage dispersion comes predominantly from university education, which explains 9 percent of the total variance in earnings and 28 percent of the explained variance (Rutkowski, 1997).

---

[29]   These results were obtained by estimating a Mincerian type earnings function on 1995 LFS data (Rutkowski 1997).

Table 2.3   Earnings differentials by educational attainment, 1988 - 1995

Educational attainment	1988	1992	1995		
			National economy	Public sector	Private sector
			Basic vocational =100		
University	118,7	146,1	148,3	137,2	188,4
Post-secondary	n.a.	n.a.	98,0	90,9	122,7
Secondary [a]	95,9	109,9	n.a.	n.a.	n.a.
Vocational	n.a.	n.a.	111,3	108,8	113,9
General	n.a.	n.a.	105,8	104,2	106,7
Basic vocational [b]	100,0	100,0	100,0	100,0	100,0
Primary [c]	87,0	93,6	87,3	85,9	88,7

Note:

Earnings = Average net monthly earnings of full-time workers in main jobs

a) Including post-secondary.

b) Vocational training (3 years) which does not lead to a high school diploma.

c) Including less than primary education

Source: Family Budget Surveys 1988 and 1992, GUS; Labor Force Survey May 1995, GUS; author's calculations.

The increase in returns to education is characteristic of many – if not the majority – of transitional economies (Orazem and Vodopivec, 1995; Vecernik, 1995). It should be noted, however, that the increase in returns to education during the transition could not have been determined based on the historical experience of developing countries undergoing adjustment. In many developing countries, returns to education have declined during economic adjustment (Horton et al., 1994).[30]

Educational premia in Poland have come to resemble those observed in OECD countries. The rate of return to one year of schooling accounts for 7 to 8 percent in Poland – up from about 5 percent before the transition – and is similar to that prevailing in developed-market economies (Rutkowski, 1996a). However, on closer inspection it turns out that the premium to university education in Poland is still lower than in other OECD countries (Table 2.4). In Poland a university-educated worker earns, on average, 60 percent more than a worker without a secondary education. In Germany or the UK this differential is around 100 percent. This suggests that there may still be room for an increase in educational premia in Poland.

---

[30] There is important structural difference underlying these divergent trends in returns to education in developing countries and in historically planned economies. In the former the rate of return to schooling was high by the developed economies standard whereas in the latter it was low. Thus both groups experience what is called "regression toward the mean".

Figure 2.10   Earnings differentials by educational attainment
(basic vocational =100)

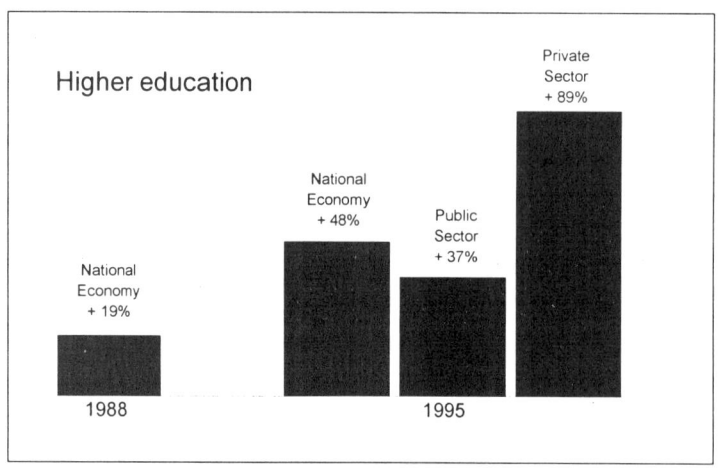

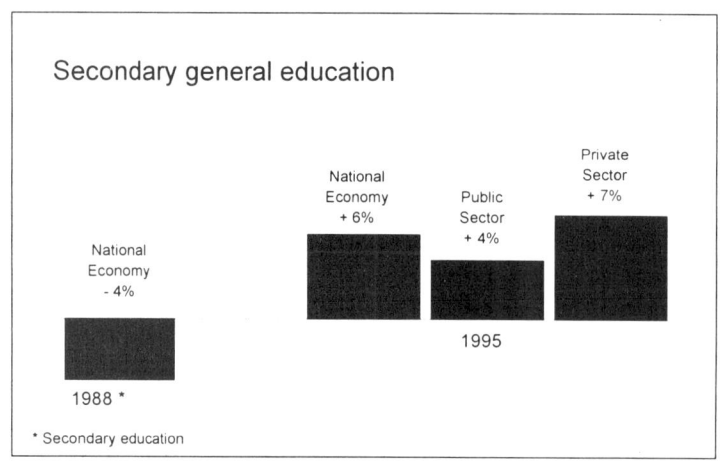

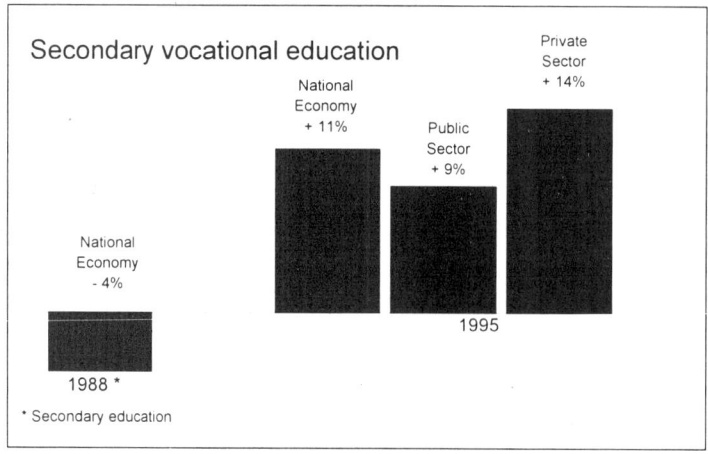

Source: As in Table 2.2

Educational premia may remain below the equilibrium level for two reasons. First, highly educated workers in the public services sector earn considerably less than similar workers in the private sector, so that salaries of public-sector teachers or doctors are disproportionately low. Second, wages of low-skilled workers are still above equilibrium as indicated by the disproportionately high and rising unemployment rate among this group. Thus, the increase in educational premia can also be accomplished through the downward adjustment of the relative wages of low skilled workers.

Table 2.4   Ratios of earnings of men by educational attainment (early 1990s)

Country	Relative wage: LevelE/LevelA
Austria	1,74
Denmark	1,61
France b)	3,81
Germany a)	1,94
Netherlands b)	1,86
Norway	1,35
Poland	1,64
Sweden	1,55
United Kingdom	2,04
United States	2,47

Note:
Level A = Less than four years of high school
Level D = Less than four years of college or university
Level E = At least four years of college or university

a) Level D&E/Level A
b) Middle/late 1980s

Source:
Poland: LFS May 1995, Bank staff calculations
OECD countries: OECD Jobs Study, 1994

Market reforms in Poland have brought about an increase in returns to white-collar skills as well as to education and reversed the situation that prevailed under central planning, where blue-collar workers earned more than white-collar workers. At present, a median white-collar worker earns about 20 percent more than a median blue-collar worker. This difference is even more pronounced in the case of the elite in both occupations; presently, top-paid white-collar workers earn significantly more than top-paid blue-collar workers, while before the transition they earned less (Figure 2.11).

Public services are the major exception to the prevailing pattern of rising returns to education and white collar skills. Although the occupations are human-capital intensive, salaries paid to civil servants, teachers, and doctors are relatively low and have hardly improved relative to the national average. In fact, the relative position of many social-sector workers has worsened. For instance, at present secondary-school teachers earn less than the average wage while before the transition their earnings were higher than the average. Similarly, the relative earnings of health-care personnel, including doctors, have deteriorated. This important problem negatively affects the morale of social services workers, the quality of human capital employed in these sectors, and the quality of services. On the other hand, fiscal stringency implies that there are no quick fixes and systemic reforms of financing and provision of social services are necessary.

Figure 2.11   Ratio of top decile earnings of white collar workers to top decile earnings of blue collar workers by sector, 1987 and 1995

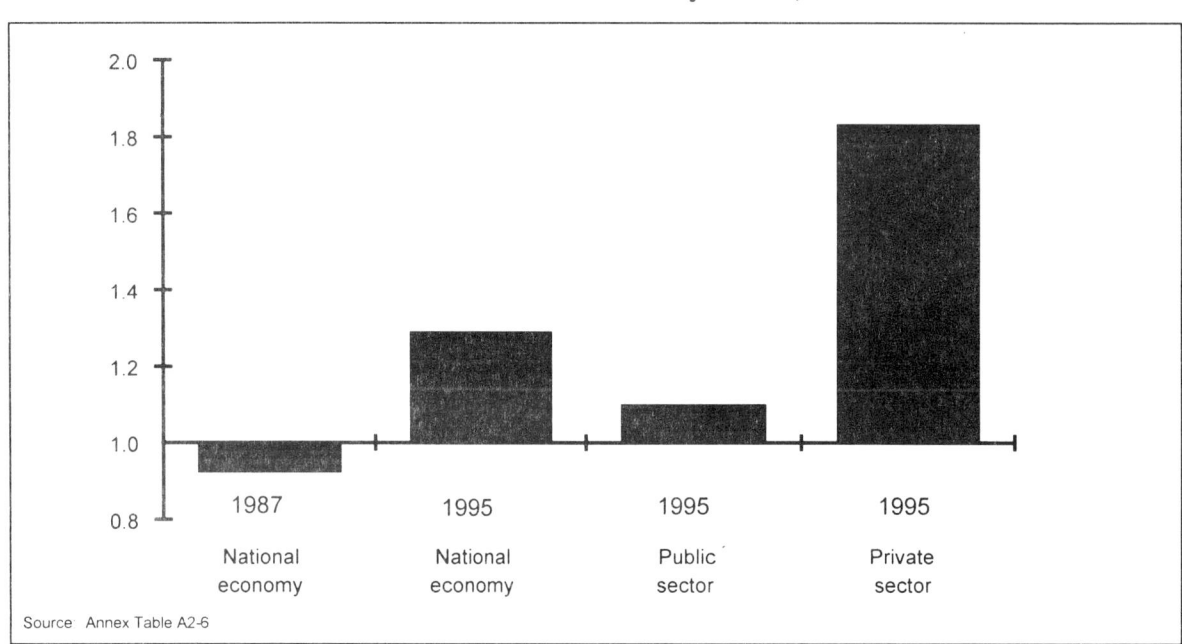

Source Annex Table A2-6

Differences in returns to education between the public and the private sector are dramatic. Although the public sector follows the trend determined by the private sector, the wage structure is still conservative in that returns to education are significantly lower than in the private sector. The earnings of a university-educated worker are higher than those of a worker with basic vocational training by 90 percent in the private sector and only by 40 percent in the public sector. Interestingly, returns to tertiary education below university level, negative in the public sector, are highly positive in the private sector.

Inter-sectoral differences in earnings opportunities are depicted in Figure 2.12. The figure's message is simple but telling: the better educated you are, the better off you are in the private sector. Workers without specific skills (general secondary education) or who have narrow manual skills (basic vocational training) should seek employment in the public sector. The private sector offers good jobs for well-educated, highly skilled white-collar workers but not to poorly educated, low-skilled blue-collar workers. Since average wages are lower in the private sector, private-sector employment is less attractive than public-sector employment. This points to the political economy dimension of the changes in the wage structure and explains some workers' aversion toward privatization.

Figure 2.12   Ratio of average private sector wage to public sector wage by educational attainment, 1995 (public sector = 100)

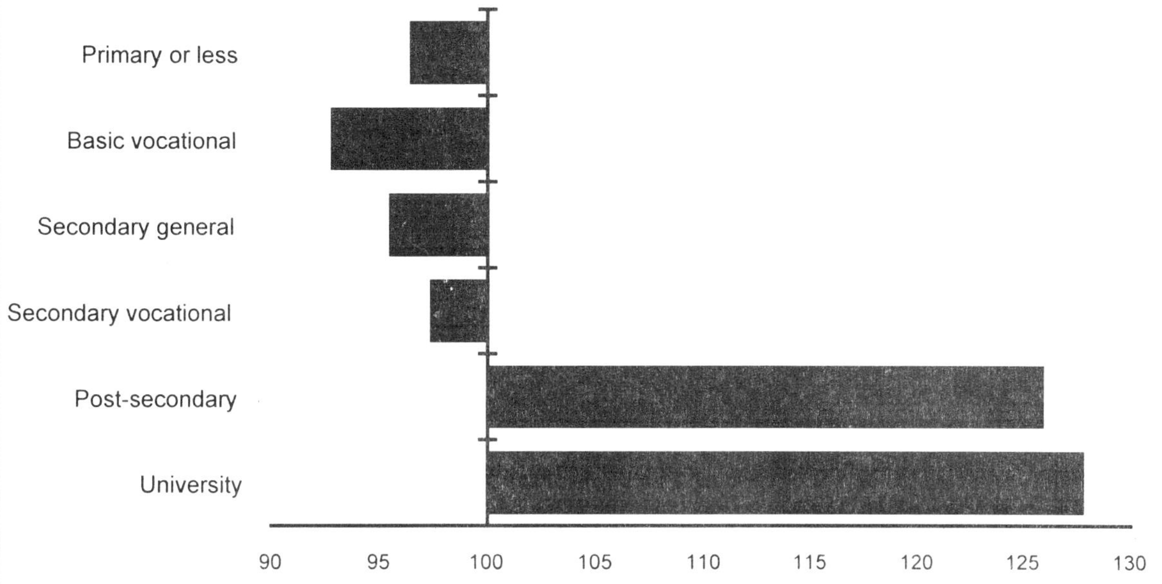

Source: Annex Table A2-7

As the wage structure changed, a class developed of well-paid, highly skilled and educated professionals who are employed largely in the private sector. This group, however, is relatively small. A larger group consists of those who lost their privileged status during the transition, mainly blue-collar workers with lower skills and educational attainment. For this category of workers, employment in the public sector is more attractive than in the private sector. There is also a third group of well-educated and highly qualified workers employed in the public sector, especially in social service, who are trapped in low-paying public-sector employment and have limited opportunities for employment in the private sector.

Labor market transition: an assessment

Market-oriented reforms and the privatization of the economy have brought about a remarkable increase in returns to human capital, which has become a decisive factor determining labor market prospects. Well-educated workers see development of the private sector as an opportunity, while poorly educated workers see privatization as bringing increased uncertainty and risk.

The primary cause of differential unemployment rates by skills and of the increase in returns to education seems to be demand shifts for different types of labor (Rutkowski, 1996a). These demand shifts, in turn, have been caused by economic restructuring favoring more human capital-intensive industries and skill-biased technological change. The best example of this is the rapid development of new service industries such as finance, banking, and business services, which require high skills and computer literacy. At the same time, overdeveloped industries that under central planning employed narrowly trained blue-collar workers are now shedding labor.

The government responded to growing unemployment by developing active (as well as passive) labor-market policies: wage subsidies to the private sector, public works, and labor-market training. The first two – subsidized employment programs – give jobs, usually temporary, to those who are least successful on the labor market and thus perform an equity function. Training measures aimed directly at skill mismatches are as a rule targeted to better-educated workers. This is done for efficiency reasons but also because of the lack of interest and high cost of learning on the part of less-educated workers. All of these measures are at best modestly successful in increasing the reemployment probabilities of participants and play a negligible part in reducing total unemployment (World Bank, 1995).

This lack of success of ALMPs in Poland is not a result of inadequate resources. Rather, it is a reflection of the limited effectiveness of ALMPs in general in combating unemployment. There seems to be a growing agreement that ALMPs can play only a marginal role in reducing unemployment, especially when it is high (Lehmann, 1995). Active policies' performance in placing workers in the private sector appears to reflect economic conditions and not to overcome them. There is particular disillusionment with training and retraining schemes, which until recently were thought of as the most promising response to structural unemployment. It turns out that while retraining may slightly increase the chances of employment, it does so to similar effect but at a higher cost than job search assistance (OECD, 1993). Moreover, as put by Robinson (1995), "[The] success of a training programme relies on a well-functioning aggregate labor market, much more so than a successful labour market relies on a well-functioning training programme." This skeptical remark on training actually refers to virtually all active labor-market measures.

In the light of the experience of the OECD countries with ALMPs, the limited share of resources allocated to labor-market programs in Poland should not to be blamed for high unemployment. The present level of unemployment is not a result of inadequate labor-market policies. Instead, it reflects aggregate demand and supply shocks caused by the transition as well as lower demand for less-skilled labor caused by skill-biased technological progress.

Thus, the real issue is not the small amount of resources that go to ALMPs but their optimal allocation to different programs, proper program design, and rational targeting. There is room for improvement in all three objectives. For example, substantial resources are allocated to public works, which are not only costly but, contrary to expectations, do not provide a stepping stone to regular employment. Targeted training programs also appear far from perfect in terms of both equity and allocative efficiency. Thus, the reallocation of resources toward programs that have the largest net impact, improved targeting, and better program design can bring substantial efficiency gains.

However, an adequate Public Employment Services infrastructure is a prerequisite for the successful implementation of ALMPs. Development of such an infrastructure should be given priority and efforts should be concentrated on developing labor-market information systems, job search assistance, and job counseling. A system for assessing programs should be developed to help allocate resources according to objective criteria.

The crucial measure for reducing unemployment as well as informal employment is to contain the growth of labor costs. Labor costs in Poland are relatively high, higher than in its more developed neighbors, the Czech and Slovak Republics.[31] This is not an easy task however, as one reason for high labor costs is the extremely high payroll tax that finances social security expenditures. Thus labor cost containment is closely linked with pension reform.

The high incidence of unemployment among low-skilled workers points to the insufficient adjustment of wages as a possible source of unemployment among this group. The differential between the lowest decile and the median wage is relatively small in Poland by US standards. American standards are relevant in this respect, as low unemployment in the US relative to Europe is usually accounted for by a flexible wage structure. It is claimed that "a fully flexible wage structure would ensure that abilities do not matter for employment: all ability groups could price themselves into work" (OECD, 1994). Moreover, private-sector job creation has been fastest in countries where the relative wage of lower-ability workers has fallen most (OECD, 1995).

The wage distribution in Poland has widened, largely because of changes at the upper end. Low- productivity workers still can command wages close to 60 percent of the median and the floor set by the minimum wage is around 40 percent of the median. It may be the case that some workers are barred from employment because of wages in excess of potential productivity. The response to this problem can be two pronged: (a) improve productivity through training whenever possible and cost effective, and (b) allow wages of low-skill workers to fall in order to absorb the excess labor supply.[32] However, the latter option – allowing greater dispersion of wages – is associated with a painful trade-off as it implies less unemployment at the price of higher inequality. At the moment, despite widening of the wage distribution, Poland is still firmly within the boundaries of the European model of a

---

[31]   The average monthly wage (gross of income tax and all payroll taxes) in Poland in 1995 was US $413, whereas in the Slovak Republic it was $ 333 and in the Czech Republic $ 390. In Hungary, labor costs were higher and amounted to $ 453. (EBRD data taken from Eastern Europe Monitor No. 5, May 1996). It should be noted that one source of the rise in labor costs in dollar terms was the strong appreciation of the Polish currency.

[32]   Wage rigidity is associated, *inter alia,* with wage floors: the minimum wage and the unemployment benefit. In principle, greater wage flexibility can be achieved through reducing the "bite" of the minimum wage and unemployment benefit.

relatively narrow earnings poverty gap (the P_{10} ratio), which tends to be associated with high unemployment.

This brings in the issue of the assessment of the changes in the wage structure that have occurred in Poland. Is rising earnings dispersion good or bad? The answer depends on relative values the society attaches to efficiency and equity and whether society values more equity in job access or in equality of incomes. And, finally, it depends on the initial conditions. If, as in Poland, the initial point was that of relative equality of earnings and low economic efficiency, then a move towards more dispersed wages stands to bring substantial efficiency gains.

Efficiency gains associated with a broader wage structure come from two sources: better labor supply incentives and better incentives to invest in human capital. Better labor supply incentives mean that it pays to work hard. In a compressed wage structure greater effort does not achieve greater benefit. If wage differentials widen to reflect differences in individual productivity, greater effort can be adequately rewarded. If so, greater wage dispersion brings increased productivity.

Better incentives for investing in human capital spring from higher educational premia. If the wage structure is compressed, these premia are low. An increase in educational premia necessarily causes the wage structure to widen. Thus if the rise in wage inequality is driven by increased returns to education, as in Poland, then greater wage inequality stimulates the acquisition of more human capital. There is plenty of evidence that accumulation of human capital increases productivity and leads to faster economic growth.

An increase in educational premia also indicates that human capital is in demand and that it can find productive employment. Under central planning this was not the case. Although the stock of human capital in Poland, as in other socialist countries, was large, high skills were not in demand because of the low innovative potential of a centrally planned economy. In fact, human capital was being squandered. The increasing returns to skills are changing this situation, leading to a more efficient use of human resources.

Greater wage dispersion is likely to bring about clear benefits in terms of higher efficiency. Given that the initial point was that of high equality and low efficiency, this should be viewed as an improvement. However, inequality should not rise beyond the point where it destroys social cohesion and leads to social marginalization and exclusion.

The more flexible wage structure that has emerged in Poland probably moderates the problem of unemployment among low-skilled workers. However, unemployment among such workers is high, both in absolute terms and relative to better-educated workers. Whether the wages of low skilled workers will fall further to absorb the lower demand for their labor is an open question. The answer depends on the evolution of the wage-bargaining structure. Given the strong position of trade unions in Poland, there is a danger that wages will be protected at the cost of high unemployment.

Summary

- Market-oriented reforms in Poland have brought about a remarkable increase in returns to human capital. Well-educated workers face low risk of unemployment and have high earnings. In contrast, poorly educated workers face a high risk of job loss. If unemployed, they find it difficult to find a new job and those who are working are often poorly paid, especially in the private sector.

- Inadequate human capital is a significant cause of unemployment in Poland. Roughly speaking, one out of seven unemployed cannot find a job because their educational attainments fall short of what is required by employers. Given that skill mismatch may exist within educational categories, this is a lower-bound estimate of the actual magnitude of the problem.

- Active labor market policies being implemented in Poland vary in their impact on equalizing employment opportunities. Subsidized employment programs tend to enhance the equality of labor market outcomes by providing jobs to disadvantaged groups. On the other hand, labor-market training is largely received by groups with already high competitive capacity (i.e., by the well educated), making the initial differences in job chances even larger. The issue of allocative efficiency of the targeting of training arises, since evidence suggests that it is the unemployed with lower educational attainment that benefit most from training.

- Although subsidized employment programs seem well targeted, they are not very effective in helping the unemployed find work. Success rates – defined as the proportion of the program participants who find a regular job – are relatively low. Even program participants themselves do not view the programs as being helpful. The job accession rate for ex-trainees is significantly higher than for participants in subsidized employment programs, but this partly reflects the selection bias -- training participants having more favorable personal attributes.

- All in all, labor-market policies that have been carried out in Poland have not significantly enhanced equality of job access. They cover a small fraction of the unemployed and are at best moderately effective in raising re-employment probabilities. There is room for improvement in pursuing both equity and efficiency objectives, even if the overall impact of ALMPs on aggregate unemployment is limited.

- Earnings dispersion has increased during the transition. The increase has been significant, although modest in comparison with other transitional economies. At present the level of wage inequality in Poland is similar to that observed in medium to high-inequality OECD countries.

- The increase in wage dispersion has been due largely to changes at the upper end of the earnings distribution. Highly paid workers have become more numerous and their earnings have substantially improved compared to median workers. Changes at the lower end have been less pronounced. Although low-paid workers also have become more numerous, their relative earnings status has not deteriorated significantly.

- Wage differentials in the private sector are significantly greater than in the public sector. The private sector offers better earnings opportunities for highly skilled workers, but pays relatively low wages for less-skilled workers. Many private-sector jobs are low-paying jobs. Thus, the well-educated and highly skilled minority has an incentive to seek private-sector employment. The majority of workers – those with lower skills – are better off sticking to the public sector.

- The rise in wage differentials has been largely driven by a substantial increase in returns to education and white-collar skills. Well-educated white-collar workers have seen a marked improvement in their earnings status while low-skilled blue-collar workers have witnessed a fall in their relative (and absolute) wages.

- The high incidence of unemployment among low-skilled workers points to the insufficient adjustment of wages as a possible source of unemployment among this group. The wages of low-skilled workers relative to the median are high in Poland compared to countries with more flexible wage structures.

Distributional Consequences Of Transition: The New Rich And The New Poor

The transition to a market economy has caused vast changes in the Polish social structure. Some who lived humbly living under socialism have increased their incomes, while others have seen their wealth decline. Still others, such as entrepreneurs, who were virtually unknown under socialism, are trying to find their place in the new economy.

Any assessment of these changes is subject to emotional bias. Some observers claim the transition has been associated with the emergence of a narrow elite and pauperization of the rest of society, while others speak of extreme inequalities and of polarization. Still others opine that income distribution in Poland has come to resemble that in developing countries and not a developed market economy. This is consistent with the assertion that the poor have not been helped by economic growth. Though these claims contain a grain of truth, they are grossly exaggerated and are not supported by evidence.

This chapter analyzes changes in income distribution and compares the distribution in Poland with that of other OECD countries. It also examines policy responses to rising inequality and poverty.

The source of the income data is the Household Budget Survey. Micro data are used for 1995 and published data for 1987 and 1988. Income is measured as the household's net disposable income either per capita, when analyzing changes over time, or per equivalent adult, when making international comparisons.[33]

Contrary to popular opinion, the heightened income inequality following Poland's economic transition has not been extreme. While Polish society is undoubtedly less egalitarian than before the transition, the inequality is similar to that of developed market economies. Nonetheless, the relative position of certain income groups has changed considerably. In general, well-educated families have benefited from market reforms, while poorly educated families have suffered. Thanks to government intervention some vulnerable groups – pensioners being the best example – have been protected from hardship. Overall, however, government policy has not significantly lessened inequalities generated by the market.

---

[33] Income data for the 1980s are available only on a per capita basis, whereas the OECD income data are available only on per equivalent adult. Thus, the inconsistency is a price to be paid for the comparability of results.

Income inequality

Growing income inequality reflects a combination of factors. First, new opportunities and new economic activities provide new sources of income and changes in income composition. Second, changing returns to certain activities and skills have led to changes in the relative incomes of various socio-economic groups. Third, individual abilities and skills have gained importance, resulting in increased income inequality not only between social groups but also within groups.

Income composition. The transition has given rise to new economic activities and created new sources of income (Figure 3.1). The dramatic increase in self-employment, for example, is reflected in the rising share of self-employment income, which now accounts for almost 7 percent of total household income.[34] Property income has also grown in importance.

Paradoxically, families are now more dependent on state income support than before the transition.[35]   At present transfers account for almost one-third of total household income, up from less than one-fifth in 1987. Of this, pensions account for more than one-fourth of household income, twice as much as before the transition. The share of benefits has doubled to reach 6 percent of total income.

The increased share of social transfers in household income reflects efforts to develop a social safety net for those most affected by the transition; the result is a new category of families who largely live on welfare.

Another group that has benefited from the increase in social transfers is farmers. Transfers now account for one-fifth of farmer income, up from one-tenth before transition. By contrast, in worker and pensioner households there was virtually no increase in the share of transfer income. Stable composition of pensioners' incomes means that they have not only enjoyed an increase in pension income but also a commensurate increase in other incomes, including labor income. In other words, increased pension spending has not led pensioners to substitute pension income for labor income

The mirror image of the increase in the share of social transfers in household income is the decline in the role played by market income.[36] The share of market income fell from more than 80 percent before the transition to 63 percent in 1995. This average conceals the

---

[34]   In 1995, self-employment outside agriculture amounted to 1.3 million people, close to 9 percent of total employment.

[35]   This should not be surprising given the large increase in social spending documented in Chapter 1.

[36]   Market income is defined as earnings (wage income) plus self-employment income plus farm income.

Figure 3.1   Income composition, 1987 and 1995

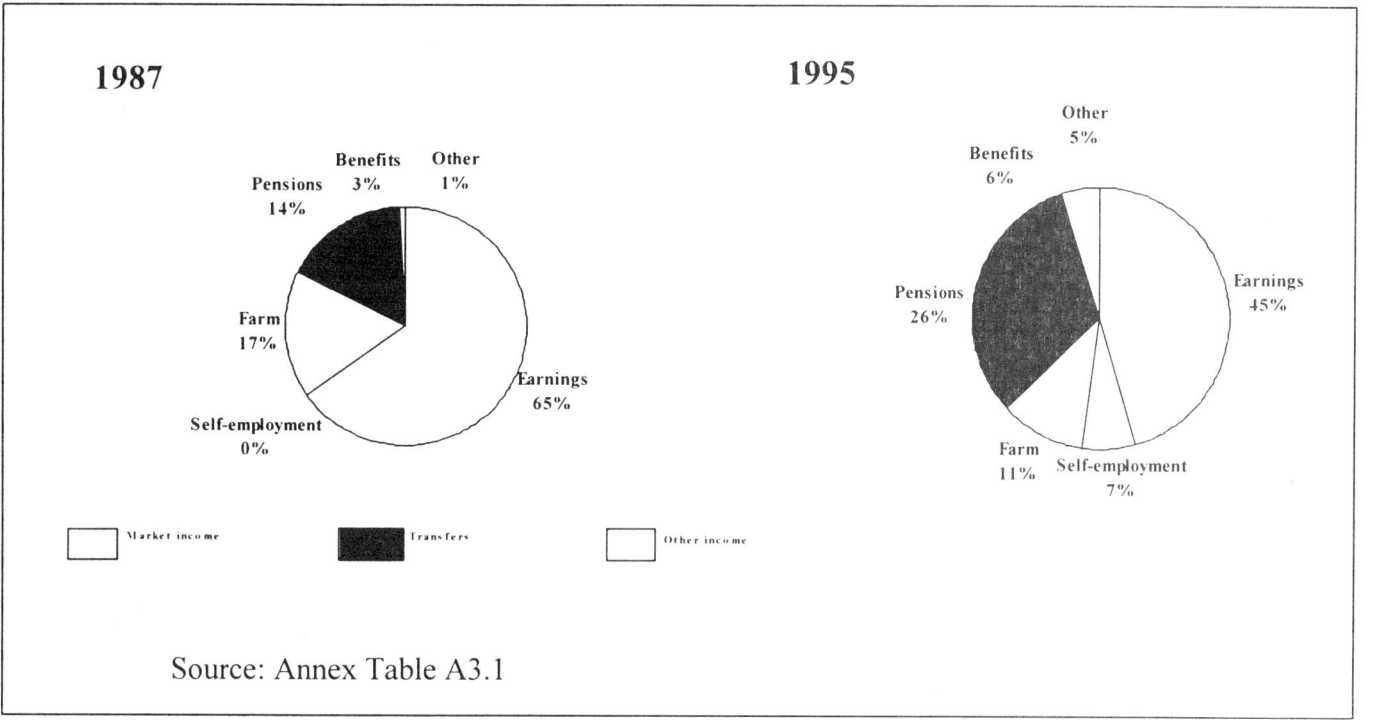

Source: Annex Table A3.1

fact that while some families still live on earned income, others have become increasingly reliant on social transfers. For example, in worker families the share of wage and salary income is now virtually the same as before the transition. However, the role of labor income has declined markedly among farmer and worker/farmer families, and is negligible among families living on welfare.

In sum, economic transition has changed income composition, increasing the share of social transfers and lowering the share of labor income. To some extent this reflects efforts to establish a social safety net and the emergence of a new category of households living on welfare. However, social spending has also increased to other social groups, mostly to farmer and worker/farmer households.

Relative incomes. Changing labor market conditions, relative prices, and the changing pattern of public spending all have caused relative incomes of some households to rise and incomes of other households to fall (Table 3.1). The biggest winners are households headed by white-collar workers, who have benefited from increased returns to education and white-collar skills. On average these families now have per capita incomes 30 percent higher than the average household, while before transition the difference was only 10 percent (Figure 3.2). Pensioners, who have benefited from generous pension spending, also are considerably better off than before the transition. At present their per capita income is somewhat higher than average, while before the transition it was below average. Households headed by the self-employed, a new social category, fill the ranks of the new rich with an average income matching that of white-collar families.

Table 3.1   Relative incomes, [a) 1987 and 1995

Household head	1987	1995
	As percentage of average household income	
Socio-economic group		
Worker	99,2	100,2
Blue collar	92,7	85,4
White collar	112,3	129,8
Farmer	108,3	96,5
Worker/farmer	101,7	86,6
Pensioner	92,6	106,5
Self-employed	-	126,9
Welfare recipient	-	54,3
Educational attainment		
University	127,7	159,8
Secondary	108,6	107,1
Basic vocational	96,2	84,5
Primary	92,5	75,8
Town size		
More than 500 thousand inhabitants	-	129,8
200-500 thousand	-	111,5
100-200 thousand	-	108,3
More than 100 thousand	112,3	120,3
20-100 thousand	103,6	101,3
Less than 20 thousand	95,9	90,1
Village	89,9	78,4

- Data not available

x Not applicable

a) Income of a given household type relative to the average household income.

The group hardest hit by the transition are farm and mixed worker/farmer families. Before transition, these two groups were relatively prosperous, with incomes higher than the average. But removal of farm subsidies, unfavorable changes in the relative prices of agricultural products, and high unemployment have negatively affected their living standards, especially for mixed households. Incomes of farmer and mixed households have grown 10 to 15 percent more slowly than average .

Another group which has lost is families headed by blue-collar workers. Their rate of growth of per capita income has been 8 percent lower than the average. Particularly striking is the widening income differential between families headed by blue and white-collar workers. Before the transition, the income of a blue-collar family averaged less than 20 percent below than that of a white-collar family; now the gap is 34 percent.

Undoubtedly, the hardest-hit are families of those who lost their jobs, have been unable to find new work, and have wound up on social assistance.[37] These families constitute a new, formerly nonexistent category of welfare recipients that occupying the very bottom of the income ladder. The average per capita income of these families is only slightly more than half of the average. Although not numerous, this group cannot be overlooked as they are the most vulnerable.

Figure 3.2   Household incomes relative to average income by socio-economic group, 1987 and 1995

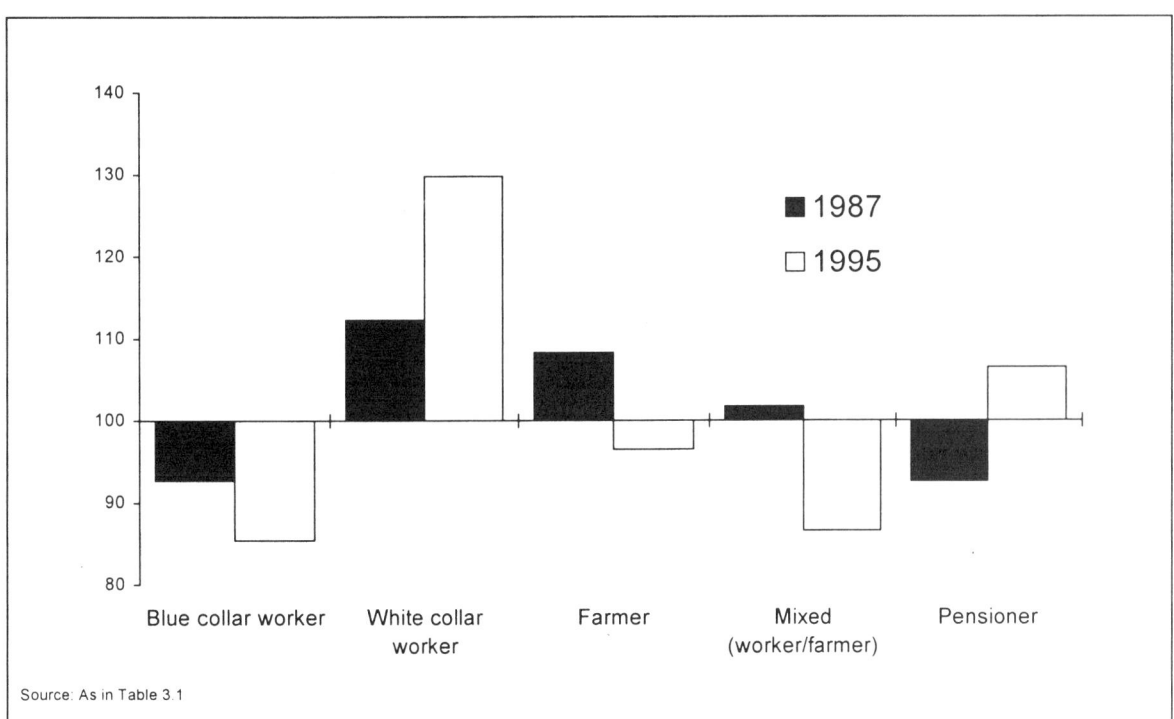

Source: As in Table 3.1

The experience of white collar worker families during the transition is closely associated with the increase in returns to education (documented in Chapter 2). Table 3.1 shows that the educational attainment of the household head is strongly related to household income. Households headed by the university educated have markedly improved their income status, while all other households have experienced a decline in relative living standards. The *per capita* income of highly educated families rose by 25 percent relative to average income, whereas the income of families where the head has basic vocational education fell by 12 percent. While better educated families also enjoyed a higher standard of living before the transition, now the difference has become much more pronounced. For example, in the late 1980s a family headed by a university educated worker had a *per capita* income which was on average one-third higher than the income of a family headed by a worker with basic vocational education. Now the

---

[37]   Many of these families include former low skilled blue collar workers, as this is the group that has been most stricken by unemployment.

differential has reached as much as 90 percent. This is indeed a tremendous change in the income status of both groups.

Well educated families tend to live in large cities, whereas poorly educated families are concentrated in villages. Hence, it comes as no surprise that those who gained during the transition tend to be concentrated in big cities and those who lost are largely inhabitants of small towns and villages (Table 3.1).

To recapitulate, a typical family that benefited from the transition is headed by a well educated white collar worker living in a large city. By contrast, at typical family that lost during the transition is headed by less educated blue collar worker or farmer living in a small town or village.

Overall income inequality. Income inequality in Poland has increased in the wake of market-oriented reforms. However, contrary to common perceptions, the increase in inequality has not been extreme, although it has been strongly concentrated over a short period of time. Though it is visibly more diversified than under socialism, Polish society remains relatively egalitarian.

Table 3.2 documents rising income inequality. The Gini coefficient rose by 6 percentage points during the transition to reach 31 in 1995. This is a small increase compared with other transition economies but a substantial one by developed-market economy standards (Milanovic, 1996). In the Czech Republic, Bulgaria, the Baltics, Ukraine, and especially Russia, the increase in inequality has been much greater and income disparities are larger. Although Hungary, Slovak Republic, and Slovenia have not experienced a discernible increase in income inequality, they are in the minority. Inequality in Poland is now comparable to that prevailing in the OECD countries, and considerably lower than in the middle-income developing countries, where the Gini is around 45 - 50 (Milanovic 1994, Jayarajah et al., 1996).

A comparison of differences in the income distribution between Poland and Bulgaria is illustrative. Both countries entered the transition at similar levels of economic development and started with low income inequality. However, Poland has successfully stabilized and moved decisively toward a market system, while Bulgaria has undertaken half-hearted reforms and wavering stabilization efforts that have led to an unstable economy and an institutional vacuum. These different patterns of transition have led to markedly different distributional outcomes. In Bulgaria, the increase in income inequality has been considerably stronger (Rutkowski, 1996c). Thus, Poland has managed to combine radical market-oriented reforms with modest increase in income inequality, while in Bulgaria less aggressive reforms have been associated with a sharp increase in inequality.

This is not to say that changes taking place in Poland are not substantial. The income distribution has widened (Table 3.2). The per capita income of a family at the top decile is now four times higher than that of a family at the bottom decile, while before transition the differential was 3.1.

Table 3.2   Summary of income distribution, 1987 and 1995

Year	Percentiles of median							Decile ratio	Gini
	P5	**P10**	**P25**	**P50**	**P75**	**P90**	**P95**		
1995	40,3	49,7	69,7	100,0	141,1	197,3	246,4	4,0	0,310
1987	48,0	56,5	74,7	100,0	133,3	175,1	206,6	3,1	0,250

Year	Cumulative decile shares (%)									Wealth gap
	S10	**S20**	**S30**	**S40**	**S50**	**S60**	**S70**	**S80**	**S90**	
1995	3,3	8,1	14,0	20,8	28,7	37,7	48,0	59,9	74,5	7,8
1987	4,1	9,8	16,5	24,2	32,8	42,3	52,9	65,0	79,3	5,0

Note:

Income = Net per capita disposable income

P10 denotes the income of the bottom decile relative to the median, expressed as a percentage.

Decile ratio = P90/P10.

Wealth Gap: The ratio of the top decile share to the bottom decile share.

Source:

1987: Atkinson and Micklewright (1992), tables PI1 and PI2

1995: Household Budget Survey 1995; author's calculations

This change results more from changes at the top of the income distribution than at the bottom. The income of a rich family relative to the median (P_{90} ratio) increased from 175 to almost 200, while the income of a poor family relative to the median (P_{10} ratio) fell from 57 to 50. Poor families have become somewhat poorer, but rich families have become much richer.[38] This pattern prevails in the transition economies of Central Europe (Milanovic, 1996) but contrasts with the Baltic countries, where inequality has increased because of decreased incomes in the bottom decile rather than increases at the top (Cornelius and Weder, 1996).

Comparing decile shares, one can see that a moderate loss experienced by the bottom decile (less than 1 percentage point) is coupled with a pronounced gain by the top decile (almost 5 percentage points). Now the bottom decile's share of income accounts for just over 3 percent and the top decile's share accounts for 26 percent. The income of the richest decile is now 7.8 times as high as the income of the poorest decile, while before the transition this "wealth gap" amounted to 5. These are not dramatic changes in income concentration compared with other transition economies, where the gap has become much larger (Milanovic, 1996).

The analysis of income decile shares (Table 3.2) indicates that the first 8 deciles have lost their income shares . The losses have been larger in the lower deciles and smaller in the upper

---

[38]   That is, poverty has become more severe and prosperity more pronounced. However, families that were poor (rich) before transition have not necessarily become poorer (richer). Some families that were poor during the socialist period have moved out of poverty, and conversely, some well-off families have slipped into poverty.

deciles. The 9th decile has slightly improved its relative position, but only the top decile has gained substantially. Overall, 5 percent of total income has been transferred from the bottom 80 percent of the population to the top 20 percent. That is, losers outnumber winners by four to one. While the gains by the top decile have been significant, the losses have been spread out over four-fifths of the population. In other words, relatively small losses by the majority have been accompanied by large gains by the minority.

Within group inequality. A part of the overall increase in income inequality can be accounted for by between-group inequality as some groups improve their income relative to others. Another part results from the increase in within-group inequality, as some members of a given group become more successful than the others. Income inequality has increased within all socio-economic groups.

By far the largest increase in within-group income inequality has been experienced by farmers, who as a result have become very heterogeneous (Table 3.3). This has been driven solely by the rising affluence of the richest farmers, which more than offsets a concurrent improvement in the relative income position of the poorest farmers. Inequality among farmers substantially exceeds that within other groups. Some farmers (about one-quarter) who own large, modern farms, have been much more successful in seizing opportunities created economic liberalization.

Three other social groups worth analyzing include families headed by the self-employed, white-collar workers, and pensioners. The self-employed have emerged along with the market reforms. In general, they have succeeded during the transition but form a diverse group that includes owners of big thriving businesses as well as owners of small businesses that just break even. A successful self-employed family at the top decile has an income more than four times higher than that of its less fortunate counterpart at the bottom decile.

White-collar families were one of the most homogenous social groups in socialist Poland, much more so than blue-collar families. Inequality among white-collar households has increased considerably and has exceeded that among blue-collar households. This increase in inequality results mainly from the emergence of families that are much better off than the others. But some white-collar worker families now live in deeper poverty, since they have fallen farther below the median.

Income inequality has also increased among pensioners. However, unlike the other groups, the main source of the change has been the deterioration of the income position of those at the bottom. The reason for this untypical development lies in the compression of pensions that took place in the late 1980s as a result of high inflation. The value of pensions eroded and the median pension was brought close to the minimum pension. In the early 1990s the link between pensions and former earnings/contributions has been re-established by the government (the so-called "revaluation of pensions") and the median pension moved away from the minimum pension.

Table 3.3   Summary of income distribution by socio-economic group: Percentiles of median, 1987 and 1995

Household head	P10		P90		Decile Ratio	
	1987	1995	1987	1995	1987	1995
Worker	58,7	54,0	168,9	195,0	2,9	3,6
Blue collar	58,6	55,9	167,7	179,5	2,9	3,2
White collar	61,1	56,9	168,1	200,7	2,7	3,5
Farmer	40,5	45,5	162,7	258,1	4,0	5,7
Worker/Farmer	60,1	55,0	170,2	190,3	2,8	3,5
Pensioner	59,3	49,6	159,1	175,2	2,7	3,5
Self-employed	-	51,7	-	220,5	-	4,3
Welfare recipient	-	53,8	-	197,4	-	3,7

- Data not available.

Note:
Income = Net per capita disposable income
P10 denotes the income of the bottom decile relative to the median, expressed as a percentage.
Decile ratio = P90/P10

Source:
1987: Budzety Gospodarstw domowych w 1987 r., GUS, Warszawa 1988
1995: Household Budget Survey 1995; author's calculations

Conclusions on income inequality. Like the other transitional economies of the CEE, Poland has experienced an increase in income inequality. The increase and the current level of inequality have been rather modest in comparison with many other transitional economies. As in other CEE countries, the increase in income dispersion has been driven by changes at the top; in other words, by rising prosperity rather than impoverishment. However, while the gains enjoyed by the wealthier minority have been significant, the losses suffered by the poorer majority have been small. Inequality has increased because of rising between- and within-group income differentials. A stratum has emerged within each socio-economic group (varying from 10 to 30 percent of the group) that has taken advantage of the new opportunities created by the transition and has markedly improved its income status.

These findings contrast with the popular perception of rapidly rising income disparities and societal polarization. About 80 percent of the Polish population considers existing income differentials to be excessive (Ferge, 1995). This contrast between observed reality and subjective evaluation of income differentials may have at least two sources.

First, the perception of inequality may be driven more by changes in income disparities than by the disparities as such. If two families (one above and one below the median) swap their income position, both will perceive their income distance from their peers (the initial comparison group) as increased, although income inequality has not changed.

Second, inequality has many dimensions, one of which is lifestyle. Behavior and consumption patterns that tended to be similar across social groups under communism have diverged. The lives of businessmen or professionals have become distinctly different from the working class. Differences in the lifestyle not only reflect differences in income but reinforce them. Society has become more heterogeneous in many dimensions, and this profound change in the social structure may be associated - not necessarily correctly - with rising income differentials.

The situation is also surprising because it contrasts with what many observers expected to happen. At the onset of transition, fears of a sharp increase in inequality were widespread. In the case of some transitional economies such fears have proven justified. The reasons for pessimism regarding the distributional impact of transition are clear, including emergence of unemployment, lack of an adequate social safety net, development of the private sector, decentralization of wage setting, and the emergence of transitory rents. In this context the relevant question is not why inequality increased in Poland but why it increased so little.

Factors that may have mitigated the forces pushing toward greater inequality include:

(i)   A large informal sector providing employment to people who otherwise would have been unemployed,[39]

(ii)   A profile of unemployment where the majority of the unemployed are secondary earners such as youth or women,[40]

(iii)   Competitive pressure in the private sector preventing wages from rising, along with egalitarian pressure exerted by trade unions in the public sector,

(iv)   A relatively effective social safety net helping many families escape poverty (Grootaert, 1995),

(v)   Relatively – in comparison with other transition economies – strong state institutions, rule of law, effective regulation, and democratic control over economic processes, limiting corruption and rent-seeking activities.

---

[39]   It is estimated that about 1 million people have a main job in the informal sector (Kalaska and Witkowski, 1996).

[40]   The unemployment rate among primary earners (household heads) was around 7 percent in 1995, while it was twice as high for spouses and 3.5 times as high for sons or daughters.

Poverty and prosperity

Three key findings emerge: First, human capital has become a decisive factor in determining the incidence of poverty and prosperity. The new rich are families of well-educated white-collar workers and entrepreneurs, while the new poor are families of poorly educated blue-collar workers and farmers.

Second, the poor have begun to benefit from economic growth. The incidence and depth of poverty have both fallen somewhat in recent years, following strong economic growth.

Third, hard-core poverty or an underclass is emerging, for whom the trickle-down effect of economic growth may not work. The hard-core poor differ from the rest of society not only in their income level, but more importantly in terms of their human capital. They are poorly educated and lack basic labor market skills. A paramount problem among this group is alcoholism. The problem of an incipient underclass calls for the development of a new set of policies, such as an effective anti-alcohol campaign, to prevent entrenched poverty and social exclusion.

Social mobility: in and out of poverty. Changes in relative incomes have altered the profile of poverty and prosperity.[41]   Table 3.4 identifies socio-economic groups which have improved their chances of earning a living, along with those who face increased risk of an inadequate income.

Many pensioner households have escaped poverty during the transition. In fact, pensioners have been more successful in moving out of poverty than any other social group. The share of pensioners in the first three quintiles has significantly decreased, and correspondingly their share in the top two quintiles has increased. One out of every four pensioners is relatively well-to-do, and only one out of seven is poor.[42] This change is yet another reflection of the increase in pension generosity.

White-collar workers have also benefited. The incidence of poverty has halved among white-collar families, while the chance of earning a high has substantially increased. More than one-third of all white-collar families live in relative prosperity and less than 6 percent are poor. Overall, the probability that a white-collar family will be in the top income group is the highest among all social groups and the probability that it is in the bottom income group is the lowest. White-collar workers do better even than the self-employed, who are often considered to be the "new rich."

---

[41]   Unless noted otherwise, throughout the text poverty and affluence are understood in relative, rather than n absolute, terms.

[42]   For this analysis a family is considered poor if it belongs to the bottom quintile, middle class if it belongs to the middle three quintiles, and well-off if it belongs to the top quintile.

Table 3.4 Distribution of household members by quintile and socio-demographic characteristics of households, 1987 and 1995

Household head	Income quintile					
	1	2	3	4	5	Total a)
1995						
Socio-economic group						
Worker	17,0	21,8	21,6	20,3	19,3	100
Blue collar	22,6	25,2	22,1	18,4	11,7	100
White collar	5,6	14,7	20,5	24,2	35,0	100
Farmer	34,2	21,6	14,7	12,2	17,3	100
Worker/Farmer	24,3	26,1	21,8	15,5	12,4	100
Pensioner	13,5	15,0	20,2	26,0	25,4	100
Self-employed	11,1	16,1	19,8	22,8	30,2	100
Welfare recipient	65,6	17,4	8,4	5,0	3,6	100
Education						
Primary	31,7	25,6	20,4	14,6	7,8	100
Basic vocational	21,9	26,6	22,6	18,0	10,9	100
Secondary	10,7	19,2	22,9	24,2	23,1	100
Post-secondary	7,8	16,7	22,8	23,2	29,5	100
University	1,9	7,7	16,1	24,2	50,2	100
1987						
Socio-economic group b)						
Worker	20,3	20,3	19,4	20,5	19,4	100
Blue collar	24,3	22,3	19,3	18,8	15,3	100
White collar	11,2	15,8	19,5	24,7	28,9	100
Farmer	25,7	17,4	14,8	14,6	27,5	100
Worker/Farmer	16,4	19,1	21,8	21,5	21,1	100
Pensioner	18,0	22,9	23,5	22,4	13,1	100
Self-employed	-	-	-	-	-	-
Welfare recipient	-	-	-	-	-	-
Education (worker households) c)						
Primary	27,3	21,3	18,6	17,7	15,3	100
Basic vocational	22,5	22,1	20,7	19,2	15,6	100
Secondary	15,4	18,0	21,4	21,8	23,6	100
Post-secondary	-	-	-	-	-	-
University	8,3	15,3	16,5	23,0	37,0	100

- Data not available

a) Data do not sum to 100 due to a rounding error.
b) Estimated from grouped data
c) 1988

Source:
1987: Budzety Gospodarstw domowych w 1987 r., GUS, Warszawa 1988
1988: Understanding poverty in Poland
1995: Household Budget Survey 1995; author's calculations

In contrast, families of blue-collar workers have moved toward the lower middle class. Fewer of them are now in extreme income groups and more are in the second and third quintile. But the overall balance of the change is negative, since the incidence of poverty among blue-collar worker families is now two times higher as the incidence of prosperity. Compared to their white-collar counterparts, blue-collar workers are four times more likely to be poor and three times less likely to be prosperous. This is a radical difference from the situation under communism.

The risk of poverty has increased most among farmer families. The incidence of poverty among farmers has risen from one- quarter before the transition to more than one-third today. Simultaneously, the fraction of well-to-do farmer families has sharply declined. Mixed families have been less hard-hit by poverty than farmers, but have even less of a chance of reaching the top income group

Families whose main source of income is social assistance are heavily concentrated in the bottom income group. However, almost 20 percent of such families are in the top three quintiles. This highlights some weakness in the means testing and points to the leakage of social assistance to the non-poor.

The cause of this situation is greater returns to human capital, as the educational attainment of the household head has gained in importance in determining income. Well-educated families have a better chance of earning high incomes and face a lower risk of poverty. Conversely, less-educated families have been crowded out from top income groups and pushed into lower ones (Figure 3.3).

For example, the risk of poverty among families of university-educated workers has declined four-fold and reached a negligible level (2 percent). At the same time, the chances of high incomes have risen considerably, so that at present half the university-educated families are in the top income group. Families headed by university-educated workers are 10 times less likely to be poor than families headed by workers with basic vocational training; before the transition this factor was less than three. At the same time, such families are almost 10 times more likely to be well-off, up from 2.5 times before the transition.

The profile of poverty and affluence has changed profoundly. At present, poor families are largely those with low levels of human capital while well-to-do families are largely those with at least secondary education (Figure 3.4). Not long ago, the human capital of the poor was not that much different from that of the non-poor (World Bank, 1995). Now the profile of poverty is becoming increasingly divergent from that of the rest of society. This process carries a risk of the emergence of an underclass and poses a challenge to social policy.

To sum up, the transition unleashed considerable social mobility. The increase in returns to human capital has been an increasingly important driving force behind this mobility. Well-educated white-collar workers and the self-employed have filled the ranks of the new rich, while poorly educated farmers and blue-collar workers have often ended up in poverty and on welfare. However, some families receiving social assistance still have high incomes, indicating imperfect targeting and leakage. Contrary to popular fears, pensioners are seldom poor.

Figure 3.3   Incidence of low and high incomes by educational attainment of household head, worker households, 1988 and 1995

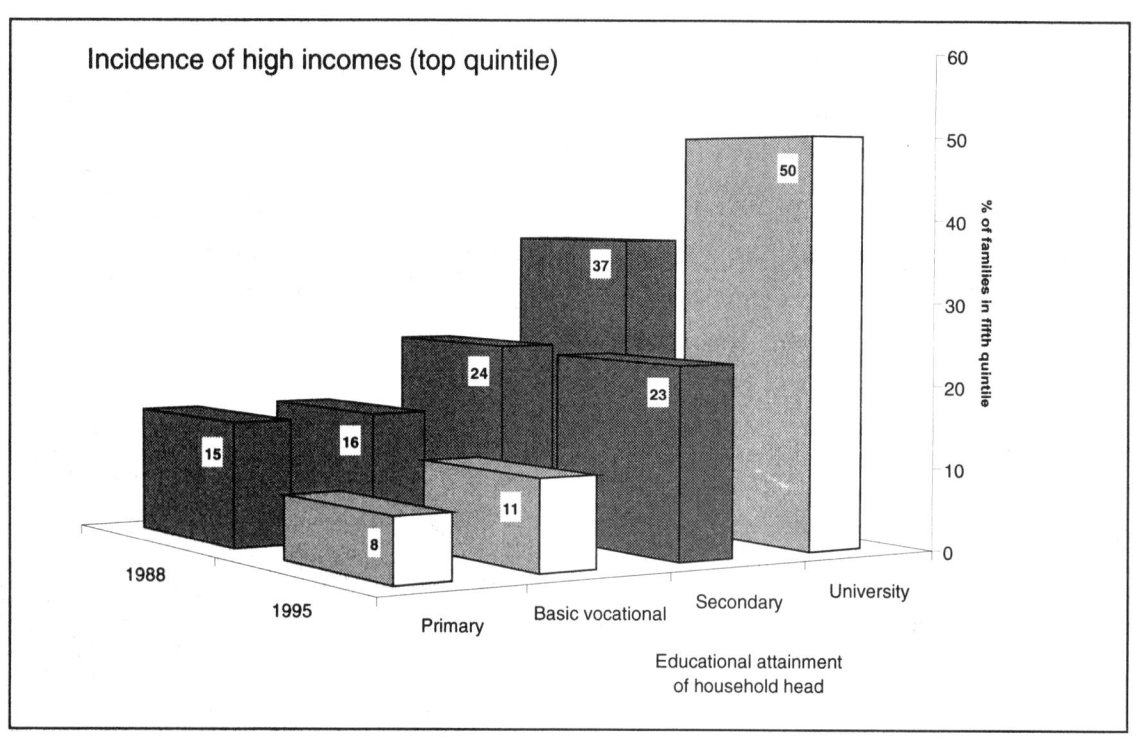

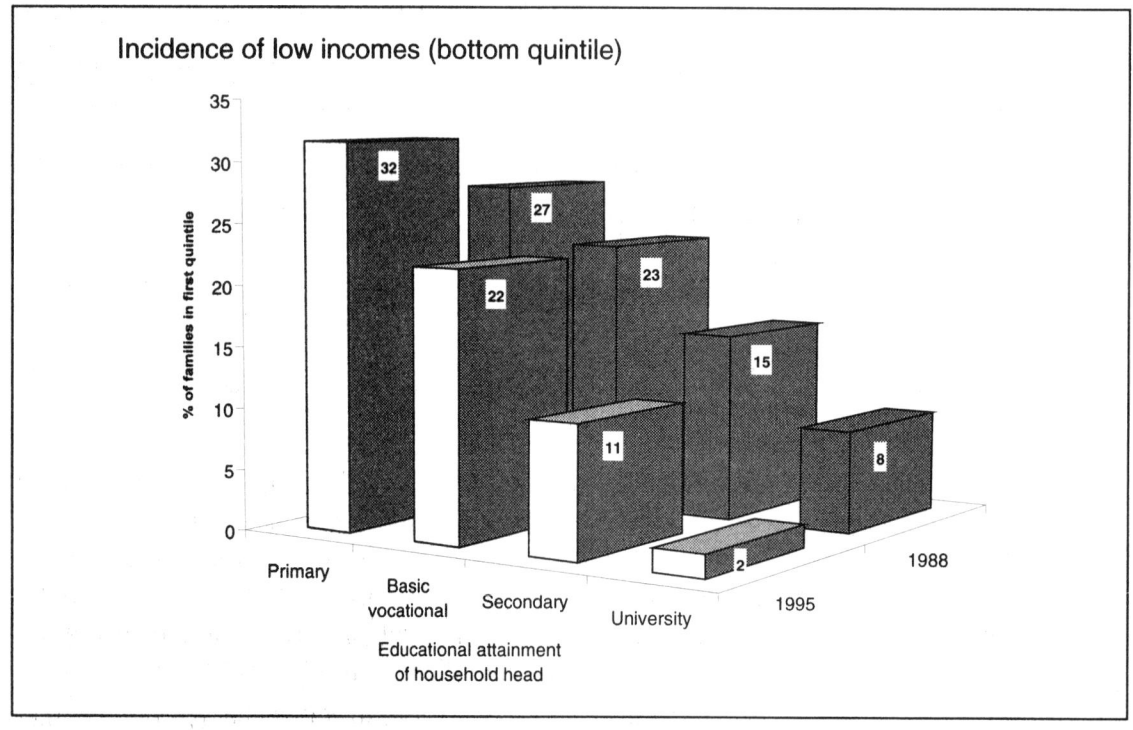

Source: As in Table 3.4

**Figure 3.4   Composition of income quintiles in 1995
by educational attainment of household head**

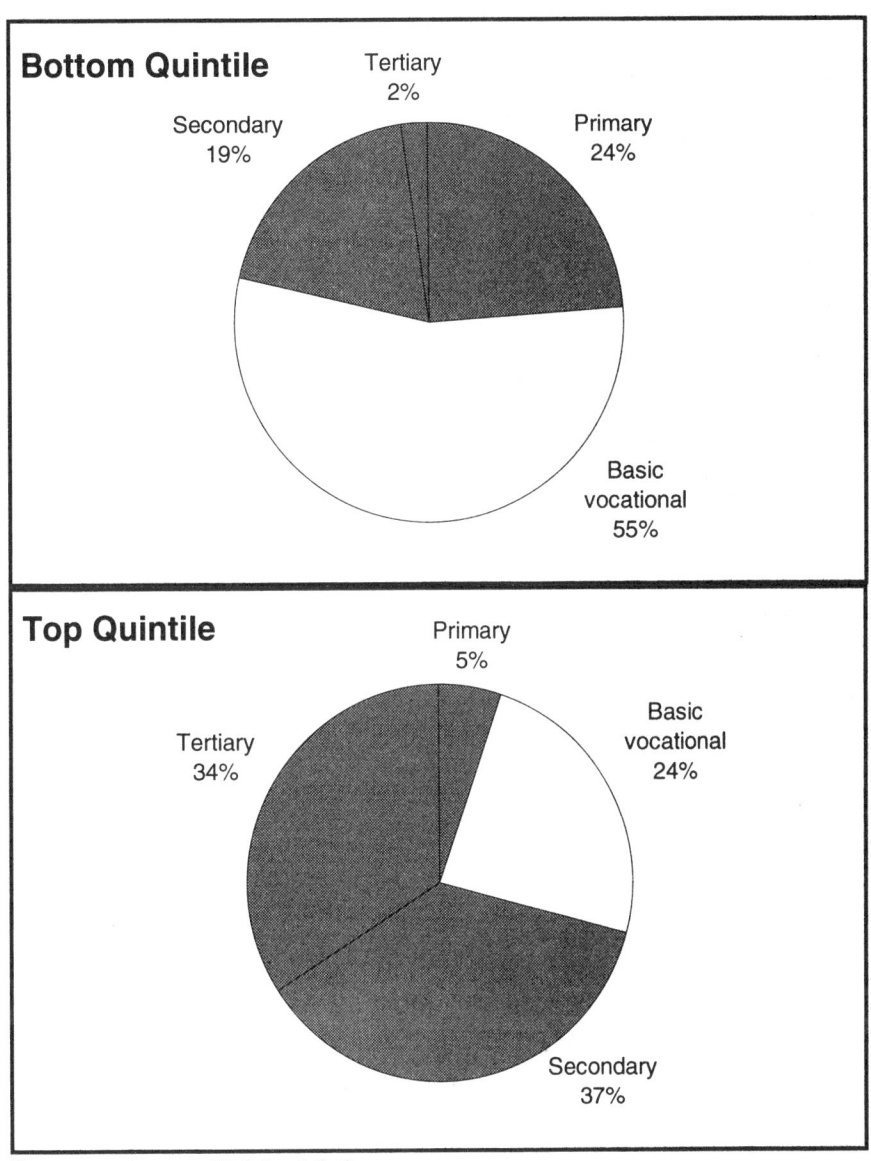

Source: Annex Table A3-2

Poverty and the economic growth. Poverty has risen considerably during the initial phase of transition in Poland as a result of economic stabilization and structural adjustment policies. These caused a substantial decline in output, a steep rise in unemployment, and in consequence a fall in incomes and consumption. Furthermore, liberalization of the economy, especially the emergence of freer labor markets, has led to the widening of income distribution. By one measure, poverty incidence has increased more than threefold in Poland during the early years of transition.[43] However, poverty in Poland is shallow, meaning that the average income

---

[43]   If the poverty line is $PPP 120 per capita per month, then the poverty headcount increased from 6 percent in 1988 to 19 percent in 1993. See Milanovic (1996).

of the poor is not much below the poverty line (World Bank, 1995). This implies that poverty is likely to be transitional, i.e., it should decline with economic growth, providing that the rise in the average income is not offset by growing inequality.

The preconditions for poverty reduction seem to be met. Economic growth resumed in Poland in 1992 and since then the economy has been growing at a rate of 5-6 percent per year. Inequality, after an initial jump, has either stabilized or at least has been increasing at a diminishing rate. The Gini coefficient has remained virtually stable at the level of 31 since 1993. The decile ratio, however, has increased somewhat in recent years, from 3.8 in 1993 to 4.0 in 1995, and the ratio of bottom-decile incomes to the median fell slightly, from 53 percent in 1993 to 50 percent in 1995. This suggests that inequality has continued to rise.

The poverty headcount in 1995 was 2.6 percentage points lower than the previous year, and the poverty gap (the average income shortfall of the poor as a percentage of the poverty line) fell by 2.3 percentage points.[44] Although these results should be treated with caution due to the short observation period, it seems reasonable to conclude that economic growth pays off. Poverty has begun to decline and be less severe.

Can the poor benefit from the trickle down of economic growth? The overall picture of poverty in Poland warrants some optimism, as was expressed by the World Bank Poverty Assessment (1995). The report claimed that poverty is shallow and the poor are not too different from the rest of the population. Their educational achievement seems reasonable and their access to social services, ownership of consumer durables, and apartments is close to that of non-poor. Correspondingly, the report concluded that Poland shows no evidence of a distinct underclass and that economic growth will pull the poor out of poverty.

The above view is true as far as the overall picture of poverty is concerned. However, it masks the fact that there are important differences among the poor. The Polish poor differ in personal characteristics, such as motivation, abilities, skills and knowledge; in their life styles and living conditions; and finally in the duration of their poverty.

There are two poor groups: the "temporary" poor and the "hard-core" poor. For the temporary poor, poverty is the result of a transitory income shock. Their incomes are not far below the poverty line and they move in and out of poverty with relatively high frequency. Despite low current incomes, their ability to participate in community life and society is not seriously inhibited. Their human capital is adequate for the requirements of a modern society and they live in conditions not that much different from the rest of the society. Their poverty is most likely to be temporary, since they have both the human and physical assets necessary to get out of poverty. These poor differ from the non-poor only in that they have lower income.

---

[44]   This results were obtained for the poverty line of 120 international dollars of per capita income. By this criterion the poverty rate in 1995 amounted to 18 percent and the poverty gap to 24 percent (author's calculations using Household Budget Survey 1995 data).

The temporary poor are likely to be among the one-quarter of the poor who have a car[45] or the one-fifth of poor families whose heads have at least a secondary education, or young couples with children whose low incomes result from living on only one wage. They are likely to benefit from economic growth, as they do not lack the necessary qualities and skills for participating in economic life.

The hard-core poor differ from the rest of the society not only in the level of their income but also in terms of their human capital, work attitudes, aspirations, and preferences. Their poverty tends to be long term, sometimes permanent or even inter-generational, due to inability to fully participate in economic life.

The hard-core poor are most likely to be found among poorly educated or illiterate families. Such families constitute a disproportionately large share of the bottom income group. For example, the families whose head does not have secondary education account for almost 80 percent of the bottom quintile, while their share in the population is about 55 percent. About one-half of the bottom quintile is functionally illiterate and cannot understand even the simplest written document, or perform simple numerical n (OECD, 1995). These figures give a rough estimate of the magnitude of hard-core poverty.

Hard-core poverty is presumably strongly associated with alcohol abuse, which seriously inhibits employment prospects. Workers who regularly abuse alcohol tend to be less productive and, accordingly, their wages tend to be low. They are likely to lose their job and once unemployed, they find it very difficult to find a new job.

The alcohol abuse problem is considerable. While an estimated 5 percent of the total adult population regularly abuse alcohol, 25-30 percent of the unemployed are alcoholics and an additional 65-70 percent regularly abuse alcohol. [46] Presumably, causality runs in both directions. Alcohol abuse leads to a vicious circle of unemployment, poverty and hopelessness which in turn leads back to alcoholism.

The hard-core poor lack not only sufficient income but also the fundamental resources necessary for societal integration. In particular, inadequate human capital hampers their employability. Economic growth may have little impact on their income and they may face prolonged poverty and social exclusion.

It is difficult to quantify the temporary versus the hard-core poor. Nonetheless the distinction calls for revision of the antipoverty policies. Policies that may work for the temporary poor will be less effective or will not work at all in the case of the hard-core poor. Economic growth and an effective social safety net stand to substantially reduce poverty that results from income shock. But entrenched poverty and social marginalization need to be tackled with different strategies, including an active anti-alcohol campaign, alcohol treatment programs,

---

[45]   This is true virtually regardless of the poverty line adopted.

[46]   Data provided by the State Agency for Prevention of Alcohol Related Problems.

promotion of healthy lifestyles, and education focused on children from disadvantaged backgrounds.

Conclusions on poverty and prosperity. In the wake of market-oriented reforms, human capital has emerged as the main factor determining family income status. Currently, families with high stocks of human capital are likely to be well off, while those with a low level of human capital face the risk of poverty . Fortunately, absolute poverty, after an initial jump during the early phase of transition, has diminished since 1992 as a result of economic growth. However, some of the working age poor lack necessary human capital to prosper. They are often functionally illiterate, lack basic skills, and have low morale and motivation. An underclass may emerge that is characterized by weak attachment to the labor market, prolonged poverty, and social exclusion. To prevent this, the government must attack hard core poverty at its roots through improvements in education, including pre-school education. This will eliminate marginalization of disadvantaged children and produce workers with basic literacy and numeracy skills. In addition, measures are necessary to prevent widespread alcohol abuse, which is a correlate of unemployment and poverty.

Inequality, poverty and the policy response

Incomes have become more dispersed since the transition because of rising earning differentials, unemployment, and the emergence of new sources of income. An important question concerns the government response to rising inequality and poverty. One of the most important ways in which the socialist welfare state differed from the capitalist one was the almost total absence of transfer targeting (Milanovic, 1995). Has the situation changed along with the transition and growing income disparities? Do social transfers lessen the disparities generated by the labor market? Are transfers targeted at the poor and do they thus relieve poverty?

Contrary to expectations, the transition in Poland has not changed the pattern whereby people of all incomes benefit from public spending. The poor receive relatively more social transfers than the rich, yet they receive less of them in absolute terms. Thus, social transfers equalize relative incomes and lessen inequalities originating in the market. However, their redistributive role is very limited and is played mainly by cash benefits, such as family allowances and unemployment benefits. Pensions tend to increase income inequalities. Transfers, especially pensions, are generous relative to family incomes. Thus they alleviate poverty and take many families – especially those of pensioners – out of poverty.

At present about two-thirds of all income inequality is generated by the market (Table 3.5). Put differently, market income contributes 22 percentage points to the Gini coefficient of 32 percent. Out of this, wage income contributes 46 percent (15 percentage points) to total inequality.[47] It is interesting to note that the public sector contributes to income inequality by almost the same degree as the private sector.

Table 3.5   Inequality by income components, 1995

Income sources	Share (in percent)	Concentration coefficient (*100)	Contribution to Gini coefficient		Progressivity index
			a)	b)	
Market income (base-line income)	63,0	34,3	21,6	67,9	x
Labor (wage) income	45,7	31,7	14,5	45,5	x
Self-employment & farm income	17,4	41,0	7,1	22,4	x
Cash social transfers	32,0	26,5	8,5	26,6	-2,5
Pensions	25,9	35,9	9,3	29,1	0,4
Benefits	6,2	-13,0	-0,8	-2,5	-2,9
Family allowance	2,0	-18,2	-0,4	-1,2	-1,1
Unemployment benefit	2,3	-19,1	-0,4	-1,4	-1,2
Other benefits	1,8	0,0	0,0	0,0	-0,6
Other income	5,0	35,8	1,8	5,6	0,1
TOTAL NET INCOME	100,0	31,8	31,8	100,0	-2,4

x Not applicable

Note:

Progressivity is measured relative to market income using Kakwani's weighted progressivity index, P.

If P < 0, a transfer is pro-poor in relative terms;

If P <0 and the concentration coefficient, C < 0, a transfer is pro-poor in absolute terms as well;

If P > 0, a transfer is pro-rich.

a) In percentage (Gini) points.

b) In percent.

Source: Household Budget Survey 1995; author's calculations

     The remaining inequality is largely accounted for by social transfers. Transfer payments add almost 9 percentage points to the market-generated inequality and explain 27 percent of total inequality. Thus, social transfers contribute to overall inequality in that the rich receive more of them, in absolute terms, than the poor, i.e. they are pro-rich in absolute terms. However, social transfers reduce differences in relative incomes, i.e. they are pro-poor in relative terms. [48]

---

[47]   The contribution of wages to overall inequality seems rather moderate in Poland. In comparison, Cornelius and Weder (1996) found that in Estonia and Lithuania the dispersion of earnings contributes 77 and 67 percent, respectively, to the overall degree of inequality.

[48]   That is, concentration coefficient for social transfers is positive but smaller than the Gini coefficient for total income. Income source that meets these conditions is called "relative income equalizer."

Two distinct groups of social transfers differ considerably in their distributional impact.[49] Pensions are pro-rich since more of them are received by rich families.[50] Thus, pensions increase income inequalities. They account for 29 percent of total inequality and raise the Gini coefficient by more than 9 percentage points.

In contrast, poor households receive more non-pension benefits.[51] The family allowance and unemployment benefits are particularly targeted at the poor. These two benefits subtract almost 1 percentage point from the Gini coefficient. Although this indicates that both benefits are relatively well-targeted and do diminish income disparities, their overall distributional impact is negligible because of their low share of total income.

Table 3.6 illustrates the distributive role of social transfers. The lowest quintile receives just under 10 percent of the total value of all social transfers, while the top quintile receives 35 percent. Thus, the rich receive 3.6 times as much in transfers as the poor. This is because the rich receive a much larger share of pension payments (40 percent) than do the poor (less than 6 percent). Although non-pension benefits are received largely by poorer households, they hardly alter the distribution of transfers, since their amount is much smaller than that of pensions. The bottom quintile receive 27 percent of their total, while the top quintile get only half as much.

Pensions are rarely received by the poor and are strongly dispersed, and thus add to income inequality. There are two reasons for this. First, in Poland pensions are earnings-related and thus earnings inequality carries over to pensions inequality.[52] Second, and more importantly, pensions are relatively generous, which implies that pensioners are seldom poor.

The bottom line of the Table 3.6 shows that public transfers in Poland are modestly pro-poor in *relative* terms. That is, their share in total income declines as income increases (i.e. they are regressive) but only mildly and not monotonically. Social transfers are virtually an equally important source of income for both the rich and the poor.[53] This indicates that social policy plays a limited role in curtailing market generated inequalities.

---

[49] It is sometimes argued that pensions should be considered as accumulated savings rather than transfers. This interpretation is valid in the case of funded pension schemes, but not in the case of pay-as-you-go systems, whereby pensions are paid out of current revenues, implying a transfer from those in work to those in retirement. Given that the pension system in Poland is unfunded (pay-as you-go), we regard pensions as social transfers.

[50] Pro-rich is a transfer such that its concentration coefficient is greater than the Gini coefficient for total income.

[51] This is reflected by a negative concentration coefficient.

[52] However, pension inequality is lower than earnings inequality since, the pension formula, in addition to the earnings related-component, has a flat-rate component, intended to play a redistributive role.

[53] It should be noted that these results are in part driven by the choice of the equivalence scale. Let us assume, following OECD (1995), that economic well-being (W), or "adjusted" income equates disposable income (D) and household size (S) in the following way: $W = D/S^E$, where E is the equivalence elasticity. In the above analysis the equivalence elasticity $E=1$ is employed, that is household income is measured *per capita*. Later in this chapter $E=0.5$ is used for the sake of comparability with OECD countries. Both equivalence scales, S^1 and $S^{0.5}$, yield somewhat different results. Comparing Table 3.6 (where the equivalence scale is S^1) with Table 3.9

Table 3.6   Percentage quintile shares by income components, 1995

Income sources	Income quintile					Total	Top/ Bottom
	Bottom	**2**	**3**	**4**	**Top**		
Market income	7,0	12,9	16,8	21,3	42,0	100,0	6,0
Wage income	6,8	13,6	17,8	22,8	39,0	100,0	5,7
Cash social transfers	9,8	12,5	17,6	24,7	35,4	100,0	3,6
Pensions	5,7	10,1	17,0	26,9	40,4	100,0	7,1
Benefits	26,9	23,0	20,1	15,9	14,2	100,0	0,5
Family allowance	29,2	24,4	19,3	15,3	11,9	100,0	0,4
Unemployment benefit	28,1	24,8	22,1	15,8	9,3	100,0	0,3
TOTAL NET INCOME	8,1	12,7	16,9	22,2	40,1	100,0	5,0
Average transfers as percentage of median per capita income	37,2	31,5	33,4	35,9	34	37,9	x

x Not applicable

Source: Household Budget Survey 1995; author's calculations

Has the role of social transfers changed in the wake of market reforms? During the socialist period, transfers were not aimed at reducing inequality or poverty and thus were not targeted. Rather, their goal was to give everyone a stake in the system. Under the relatively egalitarian socialist system, both poorer and richer families benefited from state's social expenditure. This distributional pattern of state spending served the purpose of political stabilization and was intended to gain support for the communist regime. Paradoxically, transition has not changed this situation. It neither lowered the level of social transfers, nor changed their distribution.

The virtually unchanging distribution of social transfers is documented in Table 3.7. Notwithstanding limited comparability of pre- and post-1989 data, the message appears clear. If anything, in 1995 the poor received a smaller share of social transfers than they used to, and the income-equalizing impact of social transfers is now smaller than before the transition. While before the transition cash transfers lowered the concentration coefficient for market income by about 8 percentage points, now they lower it by less than 3 points. (The progressivity index for cash transfers presented in Table 3.7). While pensions lessened income inequality in 1989, they now tend to increase it.[54]

(where the equivalence scale is $S^{0.5}$) one can see that the Polish transfer system appears more pro-poor (i.e. the poor receive more transfers than the rich) when using the equivalence elasticity E=0.5 than when using E=1.

[54]   It should be noted, however, that pension distribution in the late 1980s was unusually compressed as a result of inflation, which brought, the level of most pensions close to the minimum pension.

Table 3.7   Concentration and progressivity of social transfers, 1989 and 1995

Income sources	1989		1995	
	Concentration coefficient	Progressivity index	Concentration coefficient	Progressivity index
Market income (base-line income)	34,5	x	34,3	x
Cash social transfers	-4,5	-7,7	26,5	-2,5
Pensions	-2,6	-4,9	35,9	0,4
Benefits	-11,6	-2,3	-13,0	-2,9
Family allowance	-11,9	-2,2	-18,2	-1,1
TOTAL NET INCOME	26,0	8,5	31,8	-2,4

x Not applicable

Note:

Progressivity is measured relative to market income using Kakwani's weighted progresivity index, see notes to table 3.5.

Comparability of data between 1989 and 1995 is limited.

Source:

1989: Topinska (1991), Tables 21, 22, 23 and 24

1995: Household Budget Survey 1995; author's calculations

Social transfers now are less pro-poor and more pro-rich than before the transition. This increased "progressivity"[55] of the welfare system, along with the increased share of social spending, can be regarded as a paradox of the transition in Poland. What has happened is exactly opposite to the initial expectations, which were that market reforms would necessitate improved targeting. However, this paradoxical outcome is largely accounted for by the increase in the level of pensions relative to other sources of income. Relatively high pensions go to households that *ex post* are not poor.

In conclusion, social transfers do not play a significant redistributive role in Poland. They do lessen market-generated inequalities, but to a very limited extent. Relative to their incomes, poor families receive more social transfers than do rich families, but in absolute terms they receive less. The income-equalizing role of social transfers is played exclusively by the family allowance and the unemployment benefit, as pensions tend to raise the overall degree of inequality. This is because the public pension system is not designed to redistribute towards the poor. Pensions are effective in taking pensioners out of poverty, but this implies that they are received by households that were not originally poor.

---

[55]   According to the convention adopted in this paper, progressivity of transfers means that their share in income is higher among the richer households (their importance increases with the increase in income). A normative usage of the progressive/regressive terms can also be encountered whereby transfers are progressive if they improve the distribution of income and regressive if they make distribution more unequal. So, transfers that are regressive in a descriptive sense, are progressive in a normative sense.

The pattern whereby all income strata benefit equally from public transfers, characteristic of the socialist economy, still persists. It will change only if the present public pension system is replaced by a multi-pillar system in which the public pillar redistributes and protects against poverty while the new privately funded pillar provides an actuarially fair pension component.

Income distribution in Poland vis-á-vis OECD countries

So far, the changes in income distribution that have taken place in Poland have been compared to other transitional economies. Though the comparison is useful, it is not people's main concern. What is of interest is whether income distribution in Poland will come to resemble that in neighboring Western Europe. The fear is that income distribution, instead of becoming similar to Western economies, will resemble that of the developing world. Thus, the pattern of income distribution in other OECD countries is employed here as a yardstick. Given that Poland just became an OECD member, this point of reference is all the more relevant. In comparing income, the focus is on two key questions. First, are income inequalities in Poland larger than those typical of OECD economies? Second, do Poland's distributive policies differ from those in the OECD countries?

Two basic messages follow from the comparison. First, income inequalities in Poland are well within the range characteristic of OECD countries. In fact, income distribution in Poland resembles that in Germany, which is a relatively egalitarian society. Second, Poland is an outlier as far as the impact of social transfers on income distribution is concerned. Poland differs from majority of OECD countries in that (i) social transfers play a much more important role in raising family incomes than in any other country except Sweden, and (ii) the bulk of social transfers goes to the richest families, similar only to France and Italy. At the same time, Poland resembles most of the OECD countries in that (iii) social transfers are a more important source of income in poorer than in richer families. While one can find countries similar to Poland in a single dimension, no country is similar to Poland in all three dimensions.

Income inequality in Poland and the OECD. Poland is one of the poorest OECD countries. Its GDP per capita ($5,400 at PPP in 1995) is far below even that of less-developed West European countries. For example, GDP per capita in Spain is 2.7 times higher than in Poland. It would take Poland 20 years of economic growth at a yearly rate of 5 percent to reach Spain's current GDP. Thus, it is important to remember that income distribution in Poland is much to the left of that in other OECD countries.

Figure 3.5 shows OECD countries ordered by their Gini coefficients.[56] Income inequality in Poland is just above the OECD average and Poland occupies the median position among the OECD countries. Inequality in Poland is visibly higher than in the Scandinavian countries, somewhat higher than in Benelux and Germany, and virtually the same as in Canada, Australia, and France. It is lower than in the UK, Ireland, and the Southern European OECD

---

[56]   For the sake of comparability, the Polish income distribution data were re-calculated applying the equivalence scale used in OECD (1995).   Accordingly, the ensuing results differ from those presented earlier when all income data were expressed in per capita terms.

countries, and substantially lower than in the United States. Poland does not fall outside the range of European norms.

A more detailed picture of income distribution in Poland compared with selected OECD countries is provided in Figure 3.6. The income share of the bottom quintile in Poland amounts to 9.1 percent. In low-inequality countries it is in the range of 9.5 to 10 percent, whereas in high-inequality European countries it varies from 7 to 8 percent. In the US the share is less than 6 percent (Figure 3.6 A). It is interesting to note that the share of income accruing to the poorest of the poor (the bottom 10 percent) is twice as large in Poland as in the United States. Thus, the relative income position of the Polish poor is better than in some Western societies, as they command a larger share of total income than their counterparts in high-inequality OECD countries. However, one must not overlook the fact that the poor in Poland have lower absolute incomes than their counterparts in wealthier countries.

Figure 3.5   Summary of income distribution in OECD countries in late 1980's: Gini coefficient

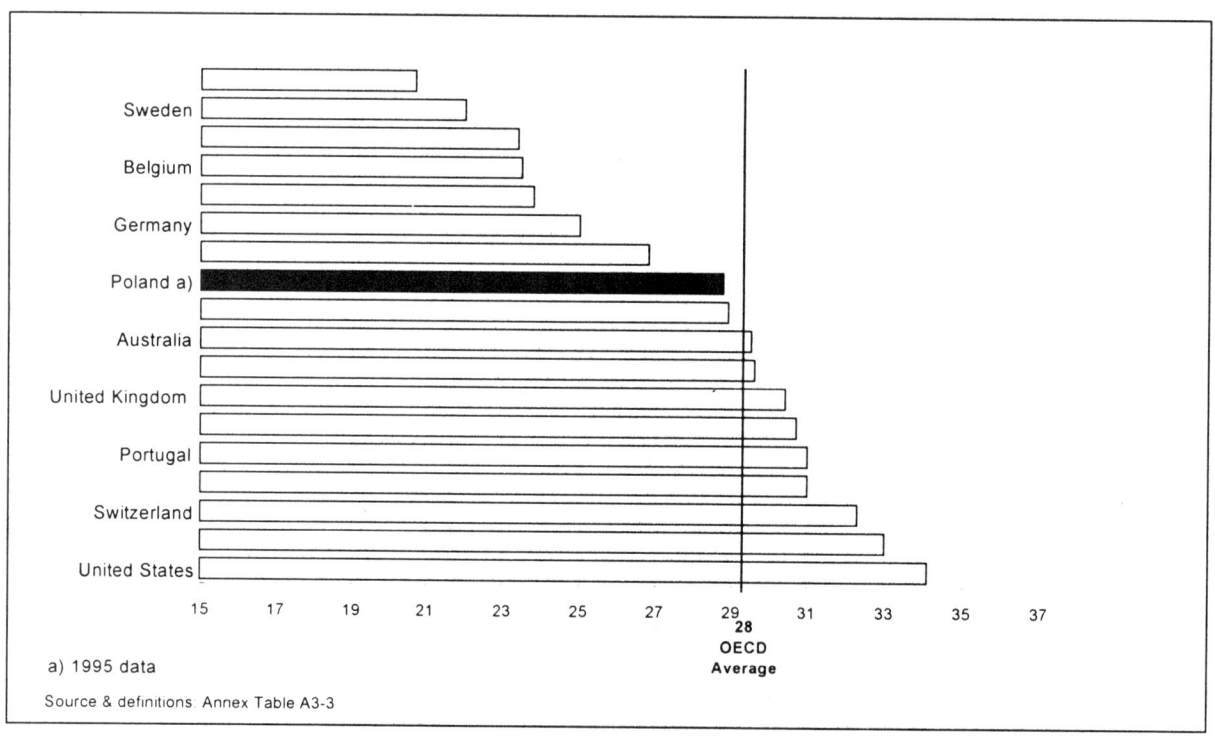

The P_{10} ratio illustrates the relative situation of the poorest segment of society (Figure 3.6 B). On this measure the Polish poor score well, too. The median income of the bottom 20 percent of the population is 55 percent of the average income. By comparison, in higher-inequality European countries (Ireland and Italy), the income of the poor accounts for less than half of the median. In the US, the average income of the poor is just above one-third of the median. The relative income of the poor in Poland is the same as in Sweden, one of the most egalitarian European societies; only the Netherlands has a significantly better ratio. This analysis implies that poverty in Poland is rather shallow by OECD standards.

Since the income of the poor in Poland is not abnormally low relative to the median income, the main source of inequality must be affluence of the rich. Indeed, much income inequality in Poland is caused by high relative incomes in a very narrow stratum of society. In Poland, the richest 10 percent of the population have 24 percent of total income. This share is higher than in the majority of the OECD countries and comparable to that in the high-inequality OECD countries (Ireland, US).. Further analysis leads to the conclusion that it is the richest of the rich – maybe the top 2-5 percent – who capture a disproportionately large share of income in Poland.

The perception of inequality is strongly associated with the "wealth gap," the income differential between the poor and the rich. The share in income of the richest 10 percent of Poles is 6.4 times that of the poorest 10 percent. By OECD standards this is not particularly large (Figure 3.6 C). This is somewhat higher than in low-inequality countries such as Sweden, the Netherlands, and Germany, where the income share of the rich is 5 to 5.5 times higher than that of the poor. However, it is lower than in middle- to high-inequality countries, where the income share of the top decile ranges from 7.7 times larger than that of the bottom decile in Canada and Italy to 9-10 times larger in the UK and Ireland and 12.5 times larger in the United States.

Using the decile ratio as a different measure of inequality, in Poland the income of a person at the top decile is 3.3 times higher than the income of a person at the bottom decile (Figure 3.6 D). This places Poland between Germany, where the decile ratio amounts to 3) and France (where the decile ratio is 3.5). In a broader perspective, the decile ratio varies from 2.7 (Sweden) to 4-4.2 (Italy, Spain, Ireland) to 5.9 (US). Thus, regardless of the measure, the income differential between the poor and the rich is in Poland still moderate in comparison to the OECD countries.

During the transition in Poland the ranks of the poor and the rich have swelled while the previously predominant middle class has become smaller. How does the proportion of the relatively poor and rich in Poland compare to the OECD countries? Has the transition shrunk the middle so that it has become smaller than in other countries? It turns out that Poland still has a large middle class and relatively few poor and rich (Figure 3.7). The proportion of people with low or modest incomes account for 21 percent in Poland and is similar to that of low-inequality countries such as Sweden and Germany. In higher-inequality countries such as Italy, Ireland, or the UK, the proportion of the poor exceeds 27 percent. At 19 percent, the proportion of people with high incomes is in Poland is again close to that of low-inequality countries such as Germany (17 percent) and the Netherlands (20 percent).

Figure 3.6   Summary of income distribution in OECD countries in late 1980's

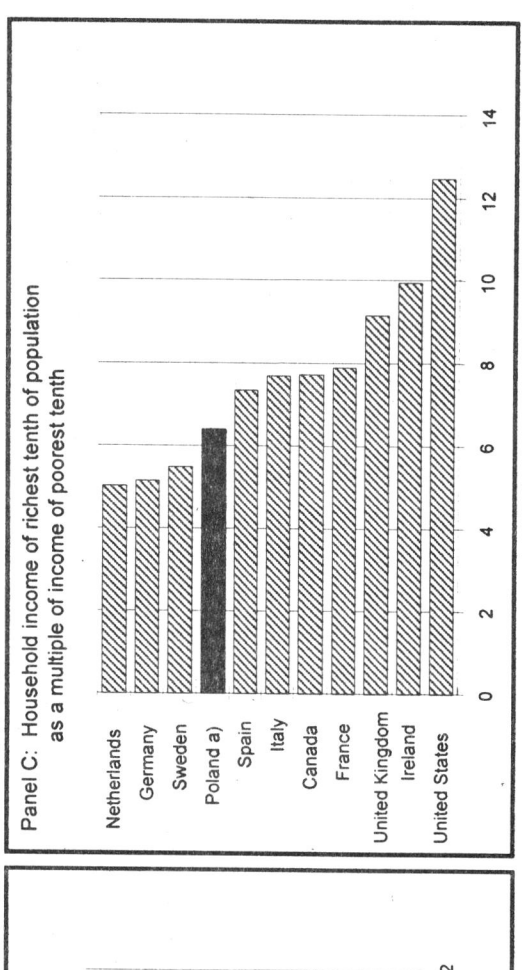

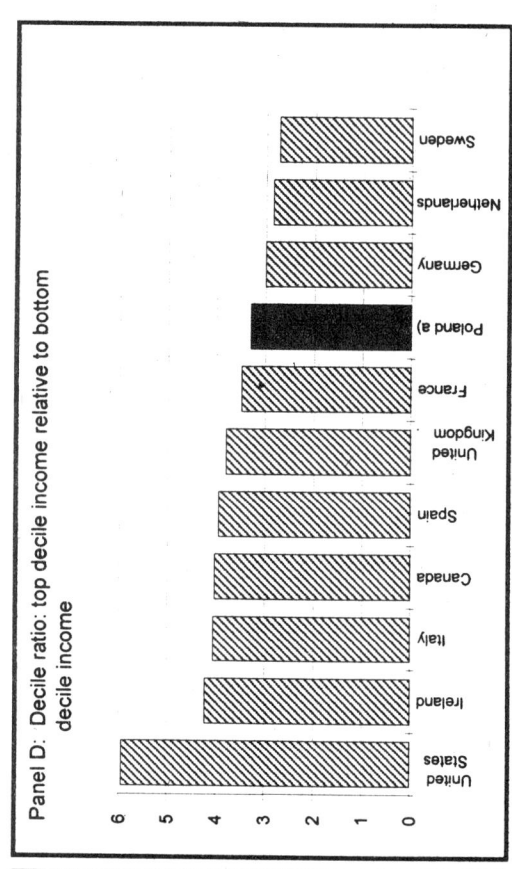

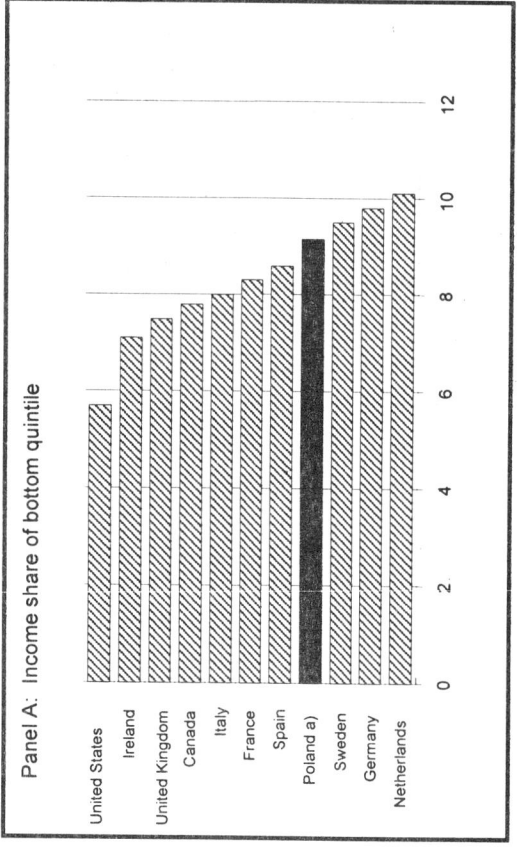

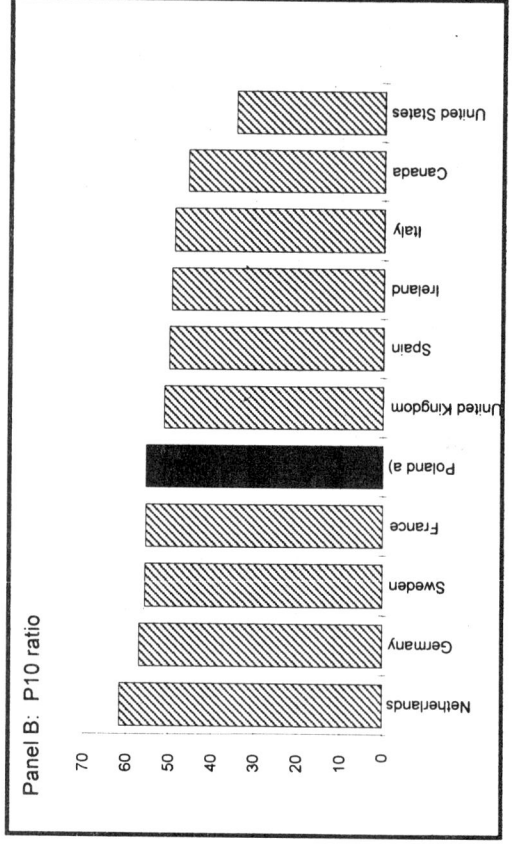

In comparison, in the higher-inequality countries, people with relatively high incomes comprise close to one-fourth of the population.

Families with middle incomes still constitute the majority of Polish society (60 percent), considerably more than in higher-inequality countries, where the middle class accounts for 45 percent (US) to 50 percent (UK). Only Sweden has a significantly larger middle class, accounting for 70 percent of the population. International comparison provides no support for the assertion that during the transition Polish society has become polarized into the numerous poor and the few rich. Although the poor have become more numerous, the rich have become more numerous as well. The proportions are still characteristic of relatively low-inequality countries.

In terms of income distribution, Poland is very similar to Germany. Both countries represent a Central European model of income distribution of moderate inequality and the dominance of the middle-income groups. This model lies between the Northern model of extremely narrow income distribution and the Anglo-Saxon and southern European model of relatively high income inequalities and more polarized societies.

In conclusion, if gauged by OECD standards, the transition in Poland has not brought about extreme income inequality. Instead, the income distribution has become similar to that of middle-inequality European countries, particularly Germany. It seems therefore that the widespread perception of a sharply rising wealth gap in Poland has its roots mainly in indeed profound social changes rather than actual growing income disparities.

The role and distribution of social transfers. Transfers in Poland play a much more important role in family budgets than anywhere in OECD except for Sweden. On average, social transfers in Poland account for 34 percent of total income, while in other European countries their share varies between 20-25 percent of income (Table 3.8). It should be noted that to a large extent these results are driven by pension financing arrangements. Countries where pensions are publicly financed tend to have higher share of social transfers in income than countries where pensions are privately financed. Thus, the high share of social income in Poland is to a large extent accounted for by a generous public pension system. Nonetheless it is still fair to say that by OECD standards Poland's welfare provisions are extremely generous. By the measure in question Poland is - together with Sweden - the most generous welfare state among the OECD countries.

Figure 3.7. Percentage distribution of low, modest and high income groups

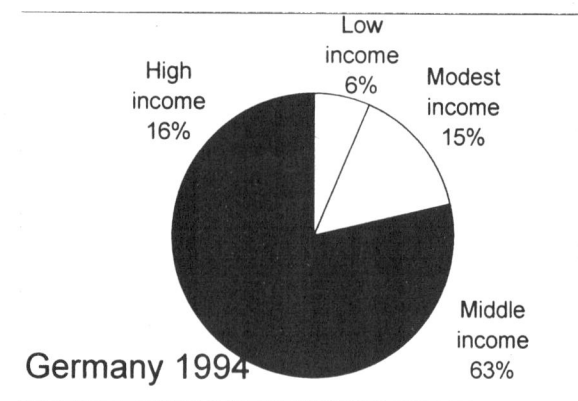

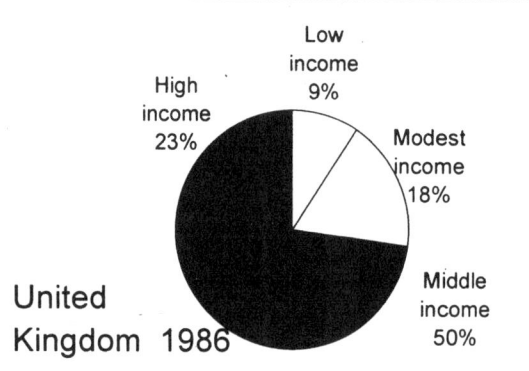

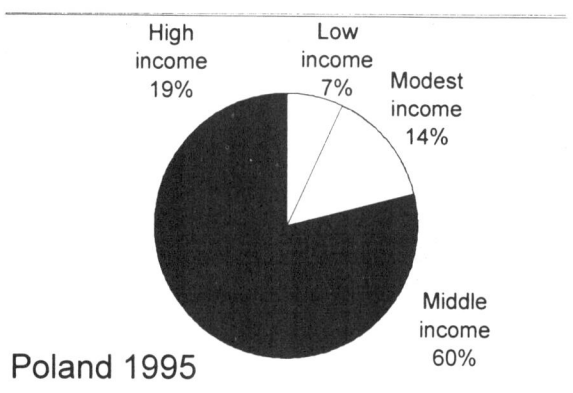

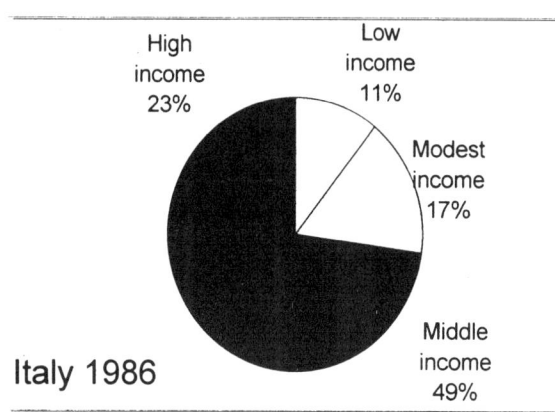

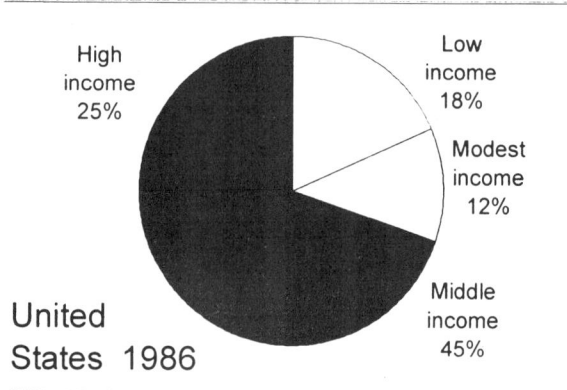

Definition of Income Groupings:

Low income = adjusted incomes below 0.5 times the median income

Modest incomes = adjusted incomes between 0.5 and 0.7 times the median income

Middle incomes = adjusted incomes between 0.7 and 1.5 times the median income

High incomes = adjusted incomes above 1.5 times the median income

Source: Annex table A3-6

Table 3.8   **Average Transfers as a Percent of Median Equivalent Income by Quintile (mid/late 1980s)**

Country	Bottom	2	3	4	Top	Overall average
Canada	18,3	15,0	11,9	9,2	7,5	12,4
France	21,9	27,2	22,9	22,1	30,8	25,0
Germany	21,6	21,9	16,5	20,8	18,2	19,8
Ireland	32,1	23,8	20,8	15,4	10,1	20,5
Italy	16,6	17,6	21,1	22,1	29,5	21,4
Netherlands	35,2	30,2	23,9	25,1	27,2	28,3
Poland a)	43,1	38,9	35,4	30,8	22,6	34,0
Sweden	27,0	45,7	38,5	35,4	30,9	35,5
United Kingdom	32,4	31,4	23,5	19,6	14,5	24,3
United States	13,7	9,9	8,0	8,2	7,1	9,4

a) 1995

Source:
OECD: Income Distribution in OECD Countries, OECD 1995
Poland: Household Bbudget Survey 1995, author's calculations.

The importance of state transfers differs across income groups (Figure 3.8). In Poland, social transfers are most important to low income households, providing 43 percent of the bottom quintile's median income. Their role gradually diminishes as incomes rise, to providing 23 percent of the top quintile's median income. This pattern prevails in OECD countries, with some notable exceptions (Table 3.8). For instance in France and Italy the pattern is reversed such that transfers are most important for the top and least important for the bottom income group. Sweden presents yet another model, where transfers benefit mostly the middle income groups. Poland resembles the UK in that transfers benefit the poorest members of the society the most (although the share of social income is substantially higher in Poland than in the UK).

Despite the fact that the share of income transfers in Poland is higher for lower-income groups, transfers are allocated largely to higher-income groups (Figure 3.8).[57] The bottom quintile receives only 14 percent of total transfer payments, a proportion that grows to 24 percent in the top quintile. This contrasts with the distributional policy prevailing in most OECD countries, where the poor usually receive the bulk of state transfers (Table 3.9). The best examples of strong targeting of public resources are the Anglo-Saxon countries. In the UK the poor receive 27 percent of all transfers and the rich only 12 percent. In Ireland transfers are even more focused on the poor, with the bottom quintile receiving three times as

---

[57]   This apparent paradox results from the fact that higher- income groups receive more transfers in absolute terms but less relative to their income. In other countries (e.g. in the Netherlands) the poor tend to receive more benefits than the rich, both relative to their income and in absolute terms.

much in social benefits as the top quintile. Against this background the Polish policy appears to be "reverse targeting," as the rich capture the bulk of public money. However, Poland is not an exception; a similar situation occurs in France and Italy.

Figure 3.8   The importance and distribution of social benefits by quintile In Poland (1995)

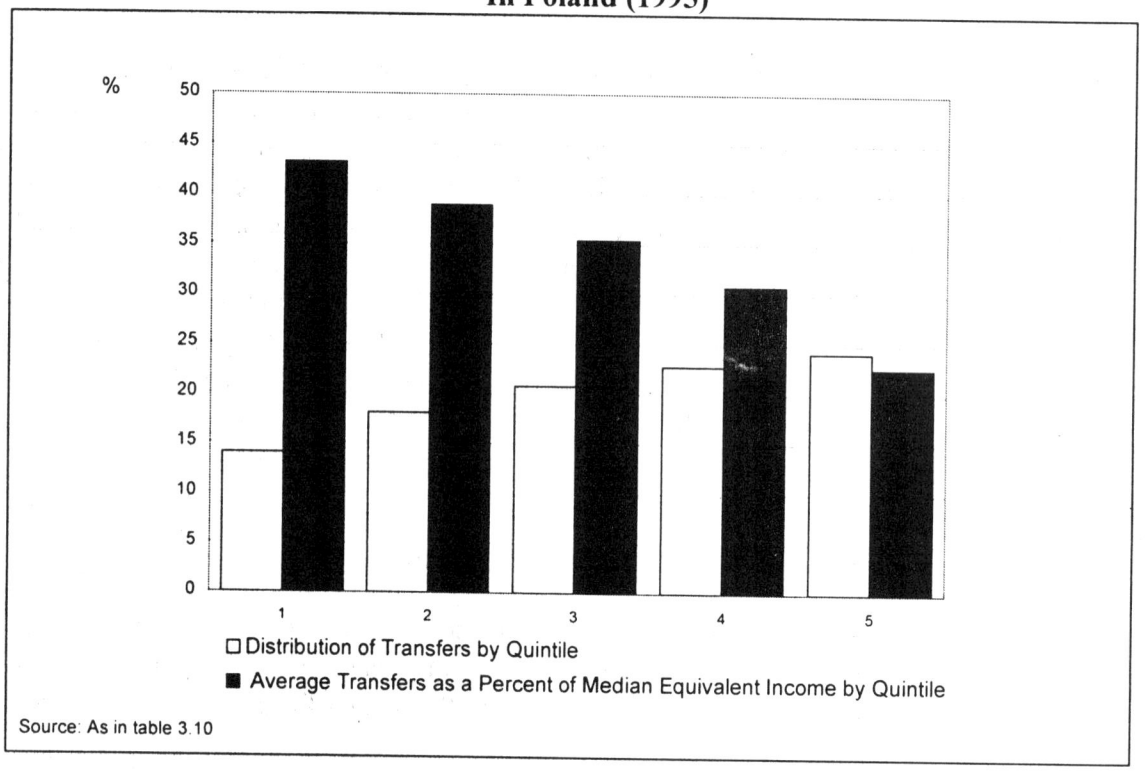

□ Distribution of Transfers by Quintile

■ Average Transfers as a Percent of Median Equivalent Income by Quintile

Source: As in table 3.10

Table 3.9   Distribution of transfers by quintile (mid/late 1980s)

Country	Bottom	2	3	4	Top	Total
Canada	29,5	24,2	19,2	15,0	12,1	100,0
France	17,5	21,8	18,4	17,7	24,7	100,0
Germany	21,8	22,2	16,7	21,0	18,3	100,0
Ireland	32,0	21,9	21,3	15,2	9,6	100,0
Italy	15,6	16,4	19,7	20,7	27,6	100,0
Netherlands	24,9	21,3	16,9	17,7	19,2	100,0
Poland a)	14,0	18,1	20,8	22,8	24,2	100,0
Sweden	15,2	25,8	21,7	19,9	17,4	100,0
United Kingdom	26,7	25,9	19,4	16,1	11,9	100,0
United States	29,2	21,2	17,1	17,5	15,1	100,0

a) 1995

Source:

OECD: Atkinson, et al. (1995)

Poland: Household Budget Survey 1995, author's calculations.

It is questionable, however, whether "targeting" is an appropriate concept when analyzing aggregate social transfers. The bulk of the transfers in Poland are pensions, which are not meant to be targeted. Insofar as pensions raise incomes, aggregate transfers will be concentrated in upper income groups. In Poland, and probably also in Italy and France, public pensions are earnings related and their distribution cannot be assessed as "good" or "bad" targeting.

In sum, the comparison with the OECD countries proves that Poland maintains a very generous social protection system. The share of transfers in family income is higher in lower income groups and declines as income goes up. Thus, the poor benefit most. This is similar to the situation in Anglo-Saxon OECD countries, but not in others, where often it is the middle class that benefits the most from public payments. Nevertheless, in Poland social transfers, which include relatively generous earnings-related pensions, are not targeted at the poor. In fact, the largest part of social transfers goes to the top income group and only a small part to the bottom. In this respect Poland is markedly different from the Anglo-Saxon countries, where transfers tend to be heavily targeted at the poor, but has a similar pattern of distribution of transfers to France and Italy.

Summary

The main findings of this chapter can be summarized as follows.

- The transition in Poland has brought about a substantial increase in the importance of transfer income. Families are now more dependent on state income support than they were before the transition, coupled with a decline in the share of market income in total household income.

- Income inequality has increased. Although substantial, this increase has been modest when compared with many other transitional economies. The current level of inequality is also moderate by transitional economies' standards.

- Income inequality has been driven largely by rising prosperity rather than by impoverishment. Some families have greatly improved their relative incomes, a trend which has not been paralleled by poorer families becoming substantially worse off.

- Those who have gained from income changes are outnumbered by those who have lost. However, while the gains have been significant, the losses have been relatively small.

- Inequality has increased not only between social groups but also within groups. Within each socio-economic group a certain fraction (varying from 10 to 30 percent) took advantage of new opportunities and markedly improved its income status.

- The impact of human capital on household income has become stronger than before the transition. Families with a high level of human capital now face a much greater chance of high incomes and a much lower risk of low incomes. The opposite is true in the case of families with low levels of human capital. Thus, the "new rich" are families of well-educated, highly skilled white-collar workers and entrepreneurs. The new poor are the families of poorly educated, low-skilled blue collar-workers and farmers.

- Economic growth has begun to trickle down to the poor and has brought some reduction in incidence and depth of poverty. This suggests that aggregate income growth has prevailed over the growth in income inequality.

- Public transfers mitigate inequality generated by the market but only to a limited degree. This equalizing role is played exclusively by the family allowance and the unemployment benefit, as pensions tend to increase the overall degree of inequality.

- The transition has changed income distribution so that it resembles that in middle-inequality European countries, particularly Germany. It seems that the widespread perception of a sharply rising wealth gap in Poland originated in social structure changes, which are indeed profound, and to a much lesser extent in the actual magnitude of income disparities.

- In comparison with the OECD countries, Poland runs an extremely generous social protection system. The part played by transfers in supporting family income in Poland is unmatched by any OECD country except Sweden.

- Poland resembles Anglo-Saxon OECD countries in that transfers tend to be more important to lower-income households; their share of family income is greater in lower-income groups and declines as income increases.

- Poland is very different from Anglo-Saxon OECD countries in its distribution of transfers. In Poland most social transfers go to the top income group and only a small fraction to the bottom. In contrast, in Anglo-Saxon countries transfers tend to be heavily targeted at the poor. The pattern of transfer distribution in Poland is similar to that observed in France and Italy, where earnings-related pensions also constitute a large part of public payments.

References

Abizadeh, Sohrab. 1988. "Economic Development and Income Elasticity of Demand for 'Government'." *Social Indicators Research* 20: 15-43.

Andrews, Emily and Mansoora Rashid. 1996. *Pension Systems in Central and Eastern Europe. An Overview of Major Trends, 1990-93.* Technical Paper 339. World Bank, Washington, D.C.

Atkinson, Anthony B. and Micklewright John. 1992. *Economic Transformation in Eastern Europe and the Distribution of Income.* Cambridge, U.K.: Cambridge University Press.

Atkinson, Anthony B., Lee Rainwater and Timothy M. Smeeding. 1995. *Income Distribution in OECD Countries. Evidence from the Luxembourg Income Study.* OECD, Paris.

Barbone, Luca and Hana Polackova. 1996. "Public Finances and Economic Transition", Policy Research Working Paper 1585. World Bank, Washington, D.C.

Bradbury, Bruce. 1993. "Male Pre and Post Tax Inequality: A Six Country Comparison," The Luxembourg Income Study, Working Paper No. 90. OECD, Paris

Cornelius, Peter K. and Beatrice S. Weder. 1996. "Economic Transformation and Income Distribution: Some Evidence from the Baltic Countries." Working Paper 96/14. International Monetary Fund, Washington, D.C.

Eatwel, John, Michael Ellman, Mats Karlsson, Mario Nuti, and Judith Shapiro. 1995. "Transformation and Integration: Shaping the Future of Central and Eastern Europe." Institute for Public Policy Research, London.

Ferge, Zsuzsa, Endre Sik, Peter Robert and Fruzsina Albert. 1995. Social Costs of Transition. International Report. SOCO Working Paper, Institute for Human Sciences, Vienna.

Gora, Marek, Mieczyslaw Socha and Urszula Sztanderska. 1995. *Analiza polskiego rynku pracy w latach 1990-1994,* Warszawa: GUS.

Grootaert, Christiaan. 1995. "Poverty and Social Transfers in Poland." Policy Research Working Paper 1440. World Bank, Washington, D.C.

GUS. 1997. Registered Unemployment in Poland. I-IV quarter 1996, Warszawa.

Horton, Susan, Ravi Kanbur, and Dipak Mazumdar. 1994 "Labor Markets in an Era of Adjustment: An Overview." in S. Horton, R. Kanbur and D. Mazumdar. (eds.), *Labor*

Markets in an Era of Adjustment, Vol. 1, EDI Development Studies. World Bank, Washington, D.C.

Jayarajah, Carl, William Branson and Binayak Sen. 1996. *Social Dimensions of Adjustment. World Bank Experience, 1980-93.* World Bank, Washington, D.C.

Kakwani, Nanak. 1980. *Income, Inequality and Poverty.* World Bank and Oxford University Press.

Kakwani, Nanak, Elene Makonnen and Jacques van der Gaag. 1990. "Structural Adjustment and Living Conditions in Developing Countries." PRE Working Paper Series 467. World Bank, Washington D.C.

Kalaska, Malgorzata and Witkowski Janusz. 1996. *Unregistered Employment in Poland in 1995.* Central Statistical Office, Warsaw.

Kostrubiec, Stanislawa and Anna Kowalska. 1997. *Efektywnosc polityki rynku pracy*, Warszawa: GUS.

Krumm, Kathie, Branko Milanovic and Michael Walton. 1994. "Transfers and the Transition from Socialism: Key Tradeoffs." Policy Research Working Paper 1380. Policy Research Department. World Bank, Washington, D.C.

Layard, Richard. 1996. "The Road Back to Full Employment." Occasional Paper No. 10. Centre for Economic Performance, LSE, London.

Lehmann, Hartmut. 1995. "Active Labor Market Policies in the OECD and in selected Transition Economies." Policy Research Working Paper 1502. World Bank, Washington, D.C.

Milanovic, Branko. 1994. "Determinants of Cross-country Income Inequality: An Augmented Kuznets' Hypothesis." PRE Working Papers Series 1246. World Bank, Washington, D.C.

Milanovic, Branko. 1995. "The Distributional Impact of Cash and In-kind Transfers in Eastern Europe and Russia." In D. Van de Walle and K. Need (eds.), *Public Spending and the Poor. Theory and Evidence.* Published for the World Bank. John Hopkins University Press, Baltimore.

Milanovic, Branko. 1996. "Income, Inequality and Poverty During the Transition.", Research Paper Series 11. Policy Research Department. World Bank, Washington, D.C.

Noss, Andrew. 1991. "Education and Adjustment. " PRE Working Paper Series 701. World Bank, Washington, D.C.

OECD (1993), *Employment Outlook*, Paris.

OECD. 1994. *The OECD Jobs Study. Evidence and Explanations.* Paris

OECD. 1995. *Literacy, Economy and Society. Results of the first International Adult Literacy Survey.* Paris.

OECD. (forthcoming). *1996-1997 Annual Review – Poland.* Paris.

Puhani, Patrick A., and Victor Steiner. 1996. "Public Works for Poland? Active Labour Policies during Transition." ZEW Discussion Paper 96-01. Mannheim.

Robinson, Peter. 1995. "The Decline of the Swedish Model and the Limits to Active Labor Market Policy." Discussion Paper 259. Centre for Economic Performance. LSE, London.

Rutkowski, Jan. 1991. "Social Expenditures in Poland: Major Programs and Recent Trends, Research Project Social Expenditures and their Distributional Impact in Eastern Europe." Paper 1. Socialist Economies Reform Unit. World Bank, Washington, D.C.

Rutkowski, Jan. 1996a. "High Skills Pay Off: The Changing Wage Structure during Economic Transition in Poland." *Economics of Transition* 4(1): 89-112.

Rutkowski, Jan. 1996b. "Changes in the Wage Structure During Economic Transition in Central and Eastern Europe." Technical Paper 340. World Bank, Washington, D.C.

Rutkowski, Jan. 1996c. "Labor Markets and Poverty in Bulgaria." Background paper prepared for the Bulgaria Poverty Assessment Study of the World Bank, mimeo.

Rutkowski, Jan. 1997. "Low Wage Employment in Transitional Economies of Central and Eastern Europe." MOCT-MOST 7(1): 105-130.

Sachs, Jeffrey. 1993. *Poland's Jump to the Market Economy.* Cambridge: MIT Press.

Sachs, Jeffrey. 1995. "Postcommunist Parties and the Politics of Entitlements." *Transition* 6(3), 1-4.

Topinska, Irena. 1991. "The Impact of Social Transfers on Income Distribution: Poland, 1989." Research Project Social Expenditures and their Distributional Impact in Eastern Europe, Paper 2. Socialist Economies Reform Unit. World Bank, Washington, D.C.

UNDP. 1995. Polska '95. Raport o Rozwoju Spolecznym, Warszawa.

World Bank. 1995. *Understanding Poverty in Poland.* Washington, D.C.

Statistical Annexes

Annex 1.   Data for figures in chapter 1

Table A1-1   Social expenditure as percentage of total public expenditure in 1989 -1995

	1989	1990	1991	1992	1993	1994	1995
Total social expenditures	41.8	49.0	58.4	60.8	62.2	64.1	62.9
Social expenditures in cash	22.6	26.1	36.2	39.4	40.8	42.6	41.6
Social insurance benefits a)	22.2	24.4	31.7	33.8	35.1	36.6	34.1
Pensions	16.3	19.6	25.7	28.2	29.8	31.8	30.4
Benefits (a)	5.9	4.8	5.8	5.6	5.2	4.7	3.7
Social assistance &							
Unemployment Benefit	0.4	1.7	4.5	5.5	5.7	5.9	7.5
Social assistance	0.4	0.9	1.7	2.2	2.3	2.4	3.9
Unemployment benefit b)	0.0	0.8	2.8	3.3	3.4	3.5	3.6
Social expenditures in kind	19.3	22.9	22.2	21.4	21.4	21.5	21.3
Education	10.3	11.7	10.4	10.4	10.7	10.8	10.5
Health & social welfare	9.0	10.4	11.1	10.3	9.9	9.9	10.0
ALMPs	0.0	0.8	0.7	0.7	0.8	0.8	0.8
Memorandum:							
Public expenditures as % of GDP	39.9	43.6	48.9	51.8	49.9	49.6	51.5

a) Including family allowances
b) Unemployment Benefits include social security contributions paid on behalf of the unemployed

Source: Statistical Yearbooks, various years. Author's calculations.

Table A1-2   Cummulative growth of real [c] social expenditure, 1989=100

	1989	1990	1991	1992	1993	1994	1995	Avg. annual growth rate
Total social expenditures	100.0	88.5	100.3	109.8	108.5	113.5	119.4	**3.0**
Social expenditures in cash	100.0	87.4	115.1	131.7	131.9	139.6	146.3	**6.5**
Social insurance benefits a)	100.0	83.0	102.4	115.0	115.2	122.1	121.9	**3.4**
Pensions	100.0	90.9	113.4	130.8	133.6	144.7	148.0	**6.8**
Benefits a)	100.0	60.9	71.2	71.3	64.2	59.1	49.3	**-11.1**
Social assistance &								
Unemployment Benefit b)	100.0	359.2	911.5	1170.7	1175.8	1234.7	1666.7	**59.8**
Social expenditures in kind	100.0	89.9	82.9	84.0	81.0	82.9	87.9	**-2.1**
Education	100.0	85.6	72.7	76.5	75.6	78.0	80.6	**-3.5**
Health & social welfare	100.0	88.1	88.8	87.2	80.9	81.7	88.9	**-1.9**
ALMPs	-	-	-	-	-	-	-	**-**
Memorandum: GDP	100.0	81.6	75.9	77.9	80.9	85.1	91.0	**-1.6**

- Data not available

a) Including family allowances
b) Unemployment Benefits include social security contributions paid on behalf of the unemployed
c) CPI has been used to bring nominal expenditure to real terms

Source: Statistical Yearbooks, various years. Author's calculations.

Table A1-3A Percentage composition of social expenditure, 1989-1995

	1989	1990	1991	1992	1993	1994	1995
Total social expenditures	100.0	100.0	100.0	100.0	100.0	100.0	100.0
Social expenditures in cash	54.0	53.3	62.0	64.8	65.6	66.4	66.1
Social insurance benefits (a)	53.1	49.8	54.2	55.7	56.4	57.1	54.3
Pensions	39.0	40.0	44.1	46.4	47.9	49.7	48.3
Benefits (a)	14.2	9.8	10.2	9.3	8.5	7.5	6.0
Social assistance &							
Unemployment Benefit (b)	0.9	3.5	7.7	9.1	9.2	9.3	11.9
Social assistance	0.9	1.9	2.9	3.6	3.7	3.8	6.2
Unemployment benefit (b)	0.0	1.6	4.8	5.4	5.5	5.5	5.7
Social expenditures in kind	46.0	46.7	38.0	35.2	34.4	33.6	33.9
Education	24.6	23.8	17.8	17.1	17.1	16.9	16.6
Health & social welfare	21.4	21.3	18.9	17.0	16.0	15.4	15.9
ALMPs	0.0	1.6	1.2	1.1	1.3	1.3	1.3

Source: Statistical Yearbooks, various years. Author's calculations.

Table A1-3B Percentage composition of social expenditure in cash and in kind, 1989-1994

	1989	1990	1991	1992	1993	1994	1995
Social expenditures in cash	100	100	100	100	100	100	100
Social insurance benefits (a)	98.4	93.5	87.5	86.0	85.9	86.1	82.0
Pensions	72.1	75.1	71.1	71.6	73.0	74.8	73.0
Benefits (a)	26.3	18.4	16.4	14.3	12.9	11.3	9.0
Social assistance &							
Unemployment Benefit (b)	1.6	6.5	12.5	14.0	14.1	13.9	18.0
Social assistance	1.6	3.5	4.7	5.6	5.6	5.7	9.4
Unemployment benefit (b)	0.0	3.0	7.8	8.4	8.4	8.3	8.6
Social expenditures+A9 in kin	100.0	100.0	100.0	100.0	100.0	100.0	100.0
Education	53.5	51.0	46.9	48.7	49.9	50.3	49.1
Health & social welfare	46.5	45.6	49.8	48.3	46.4	45.8	47.1
ALMPs	0.0	3.5	3.3	3.0	3.7	3.8	3.8

Source: Statistical Yearbooks, various years. Author's calculations.

Annex 2.   Data for figures in chapter 2

Table A2-1   Summary of earnings distribution in 1987 - 1995

POLAND	Gini	P10	P90	Decile ratio
1987	0.230	61.3	168.8	2.76
1988	0.214	62.7	163.3	2.60
1989	0.205	65.4	159.0	2.43
1990	-	-	-	-
1991	0.242	61.6	176.1	2.86
1992	0.247	61.6	179.8	2.92
1993	0.257	60.1	181.9	3.03
1994	0.281	58.5	196.5	3.36
1995	0.288	58.3	197.0	3.38

- Data not available

Notes:

P10 denotes the earnings of the bottom decile relative to the median, expressed as a percentage.

The decile ratio is the ratio of earnings at the top decile to earnings at the bottom decile, i.e. P90/P10.

Source: The World Bank SCT databse

Table A2-2   Real wage growth by selected percentiles in 1987-1994

POLAND	1st decile earnings	1st quartile earnings	3rd quartile earnings	9th decile earnings
	1987=100			
1987	100.0	100.0	100.0	100.0
1988	117.1	115.8	112.8	110.6
1989	133.1	128.8	121.1	117.4
1990	-	-	-	-
1991	94.5	94.2	95.0	98.0
1992	91.9	90.9	93.6	97.4
1993	89.4	89.1	94.2	98.2
1994	88.5	90.1	98.5	107.9
1995	92.4	93.5	103.9	113.3

Source: The World Bank SCT database

Table A2-3A Summary of earnings distribution in selected CEE countries in 1994

	Gini	P10	P90	Decile ratio	The incidence of low pay a)
1994					
Poland	0.281	58.5	196.5	3.4	17.3
Bulgaria (1995)	0.287	54.9	196.1	3.6	17.8
Czech Republic	0.260	57.6	181.2	3.1	17.2
Hungary	0.323	54.7	207.4	3.8	20.1
Slovak Republic (1993)	0.197	64.9	164.7	2.5	10.8
Slovenia	0.275	59.8	190.3	3.2	15.7
1989					
Poland	0.205	65.4	159.0	2.4	11.0
Bulgaria (1990)	0.213	63.3	162.9	2.6	13.2
Czech Republic	0.198	61.3	148.6	2.4	16.1
Hungary (1990)	0.291	57.7	196.4	3.4	18.2
Slovak Republic	0.196	62.9	152.2	2.4	13.8
Slovenia	0.222	62.1	164.9	2.7	14.3
a) Percent of workers receiving earnings lower than 2/3 of the median,expressed as a percentage. The decile ratio of earnings as the top decile to earnings at the bottom decile, i.e. P90/P10. Low pay = earnings lower than 2/3 of the median.					
Source: World Bank SCT database.					

Table A2-3B Earnings dispersion in Poland and in selected OECD countries (late 1980s/early 1990s)

	P10	P90	Decile Ratio	Incidence of low pay, %
Austria	0.51	1.78	3.5	-
France	0.65	1.96	3.0	14
Germany	0.65	1.64	2.5	13
Italy [a)]	0.75	1.56	2.1	15
Ireland				18
Netherlands	0.71	1.64	2.3	11
Poland [b)]	0.58	1.97	3.4	17.3
Portugal	0.71	1.87	2.6	12
Sweden	0.74	1.54	2.1	-
Great Britain [a)]	0.59	1.99	3.4	20
USA	0.40	2.22	5.6	26

- Data not available

Notes:
P10 denotes the earnings of the bottom decile relative to the median, expressed as a percentage.
The decile ratio is the ratio of earnings at the top decile to earnings at the bottom decile, i.e. P90/P10.
Low pay = earnings lower than 2/3 of the median

Table A2-4 Summary of earnings distribution by sector and broad occupation in 1987 and 1995

	1987	1995						
	National economy	National economy	Public sector			Private sector		
	All workers	All workers	All workers	Blue collar workers	White collar workers	All workers	Blue collar workers	White collar workers
Mean	29730.0	737.1	758.7	707.2	812.2	693.7	573.6	951.8
Median	26938.0	616.5	643.0	612.0	669.8	559.0	500.8	706.3
P5	53.0	50.8	55.3	54.8	59.5	48.6	52.4	43.2
P10	61.3	58.3	62.0	60.7	65.8	54.2	58.3	52.2
P25	77.7	74.8	77.0	74.7	79.3	69.9	73.1	68.6
P75	129.4	138.5	137.0	139.7	135.0	142.5	139.3	153.8
P90	168.8	197.0	193.2	195.2	196.4	205.8	185.2	241.2
P95	205.0	247.7	240.0	232.3	257.9	266.1	220.4	322.6
Decile ratio	2.76	3.38	3.12	3.22	2.98	3.80	3.18	4.62
Gini coefficient	0.230	0.288	0.265	0.257	0.270	0.331	0.262	0.379

Notes:
P10 denotes the earnings of the bottom decile relative to the median, expressed as a percentage.
The decile ratio is the ratio of earnings at the top decile to earnings at the bottom decile, i.e. P90/P10.

Source: Earnings Distribution as of September, various years, GUS; author's calculations.

Table A2-5 The incidence of low and high pay by sector and broad occupation in 1987 and 1995

	1987			1995				
	Public Sector			National Economy			Public Sector	Private Sector
% of workers earning less than	All workers	Blue-collar workers	White-collar workers	All workers	Blue-collar workers	White-collar workers		
1/2 Median	3.6	4.2	2.4	4.6	7.0	1.6	1.5	11.0
2/3 Median	14.3	15.3	12.2	17.3	24.0	8.6	11.7	28.5
more than:								
1.5 Median	15.1			20.5	16.5	25.8	22.1	17.3
2 Median	5.4	6.3	4.2	9.6	6.6	13.5	10.2	8.2

Note: Median = the median monthly earnings for all workers in the national economy.

Source: Earnings Distribution as of September, various years, GUS; author's calculations.

Table A2-6   **Ratio of earnings of white collar workers to earnings of blue collar workers by sector, 1987 and 1995**

Industry	Ratio of earnings of white collar workers to earnings of blue collar workers			
	1987		1995	
	Median	Top decile	Median	Top decile
Total	0.982	0.924	1.190	1.290
Public sector	n.a.	n.a.	1.096	1.100
Private sector	n.a.	n.a.	1.411	1.832
Manufacturing	1.046	1.071	1.277	1.500

Source: Earnings Distribution as of September, various years, GUS; author's calculations.

Table A2-7   **Earnings in the private sector relative to the public sector by educational attainment in 1995**

Education	Avg. private sector wage/Avg. public sector wage, %
All levels	94.9
University	127.8
Tertiray, below university	125.9
Secondary vocational	97.4
Secondary general	95.4
Basic vocational	92.8
Primary or less	96.4

Source: LFS May 1995, author's calculations

Annex 3.   Data for figures in chapter 3

Table A3-1   Income composition by socio-economic groups in 1987 and 1995

	Total income	Market income				Transfer income			Other income
		Total	Earnings	Self-employment	Farm	Transfer	Pension	Benefits	
1995									
All hh	100.0	63.0	45.7	6.7	10.7	32.0	25.9	6.2	5.0
Workers	100.0	81.3	78.9	1.0	1.4	13.2	7.4	5.8	5.4
Manual	100.0	79.7	77.3	0.7	1.8	15.0	7.5	7.5	5.3
Non-manual	100.0	83.4	81.1	1.5	0.9	10.9	7.4	3.5	5.7
Farmers	100.0	78.1	1.4	0.6	76.2	19.7	15.9	3.9	2.2
Mixed	100.0	77.5	45.8	0.7	31.0	20.8	15.3	5.5	2.4
Pension	100.0	13.0	9.0	0.5	3.5	83.0	78.0	5.0	4.1
Selfempl	100.0	86.6	13.2	71.6	1.8	8.5	5.4	3.1	5.0
Welfare	100.0	21.6	17.4	0.1	4.1	53.4	4.6	48.8	24.1
1987									
All hh	100.0	80.7	63.9	-	16.8	18.4	13.2	3.1	0.9
Workers	100.0	86.7	84.2	-	2.4	12.5	6.0	4.0	0.9
Manual	100.0	86.5	83.7	-	2.8	12.7	5.6	4.6	0.8
Non-manual	100.0	87.0	85.2	-	1.8	12.1	6.5	2.9	1.0
Farmers	100.0	89.6	1.5	-	88.0	9.5	9.1	0.1	1.0
Mixed	100.0	88.4	48.1	-	40.2	10.9	7.9	2.0	0.8
Pensioner	100.0	17.4	11.1	-	6.3	81.2	77.8	0.9	1.4

Sources:

1987: Budzety Gospodarstw domowych w 1987 r., GUS, Warszawa 1988

1995: Household Budget Survey 1995; author's calculations

Note: Market income = Earnings + Self-employment income + Farm income

Earnings=total earnings ("dochody z pracy najemnej")

Table A3-2   Socio-economic and educational composition of income quintiles in 1995

	Income quintile					
	1	2	3	4	5	Total
Socio-economic group						
Workers	41.5	53.0	52.6	49.4	47.0	48.7
Blue collar	37.0	41.3	36.2	30.0	19.1	32.7
White collar	4.5	11.7	16.4	19.4	28.0	16.0
Farmers	15.6	9.8	6.7	5.6	7.9	9.1
Workers/farmers	10.3	11.1	9.3	6.6	5.3	8.5
Pensioners	15.6	17.3	23.3	29.9	29.3	23.1
Self-employed	3.6	5.3	6.4	7.4	9.9	6.5
Welfare receipients	13.5	3.6	1.7	1.0	0.7	4.1
Total	100.0	100.0	100.0	100.0	100.0	100.0
Education of hh head, worker households						
Primary	24.0	15.2	12.2	9.3	5.2	12.9
Basic vocational	54.6	51.9	44.3	37.6	23.9	42.4
Secondary	19.2	27.1	32.5	36.6	36.7	30.7
Post-secondary	0.9	1.5	2.0	2.2	3.0	1.9
University	1.3	4.3	9.0	14.3	31.2	12.0
Total	100.0	100.0	100.0	100.0	100.0	100.0

Notes:

Income = per capita disposable income

Data show the percentage share of persons rather than households.

Source: Household Budget Survey 1995, author's calculations

Table A3-3 Gini coefficient for Poland and selected OECD countries

	Year	Gini a)
Finland	1987	20.7
Sweden	1987	22.0
Norway	1987	23.4
Belgium	1988	23.5
Luxembourg	1985	23.8
Germany	1984	25.0
Netherlands	1987	26.8
Poland	1995	28.8
Canada	1987	28.9
Australia	1985	29.5
France	1984	29.6
UK	1986	30.4
Spain	1990/91	30.7
Italy	1986	31.0
Portugal	1989/90	31.0
Switzerland	1982	32.3
Ireland	1987	33.0
United States	1986	34.1
OECD average [a]		28.0

Note: The Gini coefficiet is calculated for net disposable income per equivalent adult. The equivalence scale is that applied in OECD (1995).

a) Unewighted average for 18 countries.

Sources:
OECD: Atkinson, et al. (1995)
Poland: Household Budget Survey 1995, author's calculations.

Table A3-4   Summary of income distribution in Poland and OECD countries: cummulative decile shares and wealth gap (mid/late 1980s)

	S10	S20	S30	S40	S50	S60	S70	S80	S90	S95	Wealth gap
Poland a)	3.8	9.1	15.5	22.8	30.9	40.0	50.2	61.9	75.8	84.5	6.4
Canada	2.8	7.8	14.1	21.5	30.1	39.8	50.7	63.3	78.4	87.5	7.7
France	3.0	8.3	14.6	21.8	29.9	39.1	49.5	61.6	76.3	85.5	7.9
Germany	4.0	9.8	16.6	24.2	32.9	42.5	53.2	65.3	79.4	87.8	5.2
Ireland	2.5	7.1	12.6	19.3	27.1	36.3	47.0	59.6	75.1	84.7	10.0
Italy	3.1	8.0	13.9	20.7	28.7	38.0	48.7	61.2	76.2	85.4	7.7
Netherlands	4.1	10.1	16.9	24.5	33.0	42.5	53.2	65.3	79.4	87.8	5.0
Spain	3.3	8.6	14.6	21.6	29.6	38.6	49.0	61.2	75.8	-	7.3
Sweden	3.3	9.5	16.9	25.3	34.6	44.8	55.9	68.2	81.9	89.7	5.5
UK·	2.5	7.5	13.5	20.5	28.7	38.2	49.1	61.8	77.1	86.4	9.2
US	1.9	5.7	1.2	18.0	26.2	35.7	46.9	60.2	76.3	86.2	12.5

- Data not available

Notes:
Distribution among persons of disposable household income per equivalent adult
The equivalence scale is·the square root of the household size
Wealth Gap: The ratio of the top decile share to the bottom decile share.

a) 1995

Sources:
OECD: Atkinson, et al. (1995)
Poland: Household Budget Survey 1995, author's calculations.

Table A3-5   Summary of income distribution in Poland and OECD countries: percentiles of median (mid/late 1980s)

	P10	P25	P75	P90	P95	Decile ratio
Poland a)	55.4	74.4	135.5	182.5	227.0	3.3
Canada	45.8	68.5	137.5	184.2	218.0	4.0
France	55.4	72.1	139.7	192.8	233.5	3.5
Germany	56.9	75.0	132.7	170.8	201.7	3.0
Ireland	49.5	66.7	150.9	209.2	252.2	4.2
Italy	48.9	68.8	145.0	197.9	233.8	4.0
Netherlands	61.5	75.7	135.0	175.0	206.4	2.8
Spain	50.1	69.3	143.2	197.9	243.8	4.0
Sweden	55.6	75.6	125.1	151.5	170.4	2.7
UK	51.1	67.6	144.6	194.1	232.1	3.8
US	34.7	61.7	149.6	206.1	247.3	5.9

Notes:
Distribution among persons of disposable household income per equivalent adult.
The equivalence scale is the square root of the household size
The decile ratio = P90/P10

a) 1995

Sources:
OECD: Atkinson, et al. (1995)
Poland: Household Budget Survey 1995, author's calculations.

Table A3-6   Percentage distribution of low, modest, middle and high income groups (mid/late 1980s)

Country	Low income	Modest income	Low and modest	Middle income	High income
Poland a)	6.9	14.1	21.0	60.4	18.5
Canada	12.2	14.0	26.2	54.3	19.5
France	7.5	15.3	22.8	56.1	21.0
Germany	6.5	15.0	21.5	62.1	16.5
Ireland	10.7	16.7	27.4	47.2	25.3
Italy	10.5	16.7	27.2	49.4	23.4
Netherlands	4.9	11.5	16.4	63.2	20.4
Sweden	7.6	12.4	20.0	69.5	10.5
UK	9.1	18.1	27.2	50.0	22.8
US	18.4	11.9	30.3	44.8	24.9

Definition of income groupings:

Low income = adjusted incomes below 0.5 times median income

Modest income = adjusted incmes between 0.5 and 0.7 times median inocme;

Middle income = adjusted incomes between 0.7 and 1.5 times median income; and

High income = adjusted income above 1.5 times median income.

a) 1995

Sources:

OECD: Atkinson, et al. (1995)

Poland: Household Budget Survey 1995, author's calculations.

Distributors of World Bank Publications

Prices and credit terms vary from country to country. Consult your local distributor before placing an order.

ARGENTINA
Oficina del Libro Internacional
Av. Cordoba 1877
1120 Buenos Aires
Tel: (54 11) 815-8354
Fax: (54 11) 815-8156
E-mail: olilibro@satlink.com

AUSTRALIA, FIJI, PAPUA NEW GUINEA, SOLOMON ISLANDS, VANUATU, AND SAMOA
D.A. Information Services
648 Whitehorse Road
Mitcham 3132
Victoria
Tel: (61) 3 9210 7777
Fax: (61) 3 9210 7788
E-mail: service@dadirect.com.au

AUSTRIA
Gerold and Co.
Weihburggasse 26
A-1011 Wien
Tel: (43 1) 512-47-31-0
Fax: (43 1) 512-47-31-29

BANGLADESH
Micro Industries Development
Assistance Society (MIDAS)
House 5, Road 16
Dhanmondi R/Area
Dhaka 1209
Tel: (880 2) 326427
Fax: (880 2) 811188

BELGIUM
Jean De Lannoy
Av. du Roi 202
1060 Brussels
Tel: (32 2) 538-5169
Fax: (32 2) 538-0841

BRAZIL
Publicações Tecnicas Internacionais Ltda.
Rua Peixoto Gomide, 209
01409 Sao Paulo, SP
Tel: (55 11) 259-6644
Fax: (55 11) 258-6990
E-mail: postmaster@pti.uol.br

CANADA
Renouf Publishing Co. Ltd.
5369 Canotek Road
Ottawa, Ontario K1J 9J3
Tel: (613) 745-2665
Fax: (613) 745-7660
E-mail: order.dept@renoufbooks.com

CHINA
China Financial & Economic
Publishing House
8, Da Fo Si Dong Jie
Beijing
Tel: (86 10) 6333-8257
Fax: (86 10) 6401-7365
China Book Import Centre
P.O. Box 2825
Beijing

COLOMBIA
Infoenlace Ltda.
Carrera 6 No. 51-21
Apartado Aereo 34270
Santafé de Bogotá, D.C.
Tel: (57 1) 285-2798
Fax: (57 1) 285-2798

COTE D'IVOIRE
Center d'Edition et de Diffusion Africaines
(CEDA)
04 B.P. 541
Abidjan 04
Tel: (225) 24 6510; 24 6511
Fax: (225) 25 0567

CYPRUS
Center for Applied Research
Cyprus College
6, Diogenes Street, Engomi
P.O. Box 2006
Nicosia
Tel: (357 2) 44-1730
Fax: (357 2) 46-2051

CZECH REPUBLIC
USIS, NIS Prodejna
Havelkova 22
130 00 Prague 3
Tel: (420 2) 2423 1486
Fax: (420 2) 2423 1114

DENMARK
SamfundsLitteratur
Rosenoerns Allé 11
DK-1970 Frederiksberg C
Tel: (45 31) 351942
Fax: (45 31) 357822

ECUADOR
Libri Mundi
Librería Internacional
P.O. Box 17-01-3029
Juan Leon Mera 851
Quito
Tel/Fax: (593 2) 521-606; (593 2) 544-185
Fax: (593 2) 504-209
E-mail: librimu1@librimundi.com.ec
CODEU
Ruiz de Castilla 763, Edif. Expocolor
Primer piso, Of. #2
Quito
Tel: (593 2) 507-363; 253-091
E-mail: codeu@impsat.net.ec

EGYPT, ARAB REPUBLIC OF
Al Ahram Distribution Agency
Al Galaa Street
Cairo
Tel: (20 2) 578-6083
Fax: (20 2) 578-6833
The Middle East Observer
41, Sherif Street
Cairo
Tel: (20 2) 393-9732
Fax: (20 2) 393-9732

FINLAND
Akateeminen Kirjakauppa
P.O. Box 128
FIN-00101 Helsinki
Tel: (358 0) 121 4418
Fax: (358 0) 121-4435
E-mail: akatilaus@stockmann.fi

FRANCE
World Bank Publications
66, avenue d'Iena
75116 Paris
Tel: (33 1) 40-69-30-56/57
Fax: (33 1) 40-69-30-68

GERMANY
UNO-Verlag
Poppelsdorfer Allee 55
53115 Bonn
Tel: (49 228) 949020
Fax: (49 228) 217492
E-mail: unoverlag@aol.com

GHANA
Epp Books Services
P.O. Box 44
TUC
Accra

GREECE
Papasotiriou S.A.
35, Stournara Str.
106 82 Athens
Tel: (30 1) 364-1826
Fax: (30 1) 364-8254

HAITI
Culture Diffusion
5, Rue Capois
C.P. 257
Port-au-Prince
Tel: (509) 23 9260
Fax: (509) 23 4858

HONG KONG, CHINA; MACAO
Asia 2000 Ltd.
Sales & Circulation Department
Seabird House, unit 1101-02
22-28 Wyndham Street, Central
Hong Kong
Tel: (852) 2530-1409
Fax: (852) 2526-1107
E-mail: sales@asia2000.com.hk

HUNGARY
Euro Info Service
Margitszgeti Europa Haz
H-1138 Budapest
Tel: (36 1) 350 80 24, 350 80 25
Fax: (36 1) 350 90 32
E-mail: euroinfo@mail.matav.hu

INDIA
Allied Publishers Ltd.
751 Mount Road
Madras – 600 002
Tel: (91 44) 852-3938
Fax: (91 44) 852-0649

INDONESIA
Pt. Indira Limited
Jalan Borobudur 20
P.O. Box 181
Jakarta 10320
Tel: (62 21) 390-4290
Fax: (62 21) 390-4289

IRAN
Ketab Sara Co. Publishers
Khaled Estamboli Ave., 6th Street
Delafrooz Alley No. 8
P.O. Box 15745-733
Tehran 15117
Tel: (98 21) 8717819; 8716104
Fax: (98 21) 8712479
E-mail: ketab-sara@neda.net.ir
Kowkab Publishers
P.O. Box 19575-511
Tehran
Tel: (98 21) 258-3723
Fax: (98 21) 258-3723

IRELAND
Government Supplies Agency
Oifig an tSoláthair
4-5 Harcourt Road
Dublin 2
Tel: (353 1) 661-3111
Fax: (353 1) 475-2670

ISRAEL
Yozmot Literature Ltd.
P.O. Box 56055
3 Yohanan Hasandlar Street
Tel Aviv 61560
Tel: (972 3) 5285-397
Fax: (972 3) 5285-397
R.O.Y. International
PO Box 13056
Tel Aviv 61130
Tel: (972 3) 5461423
Fax: (972 3) 5461442
E-mail: royil@netvision.net.il
Palestinian Authority/Middle East
Index Information Services
P.O.B. 19502 Jerusalem
Tel: (972 2) 6271219
Fax: (972 2) 6271634

ITALY
Licosa Commissionaria Sansoni SPA
Via Duca Di Calabria, 1/1
Casella Postale 552
50125 Firenze
Tel: (55) 645-415
Fax: (55) 641-257
E-mail: licosa@ftbcc.it

JAMAICA
Ian Randle Publishers Ltd.
206 Old Hope Road, Kingston 6
Tel: 876-927-2085
Fax: 876-977-0243
E-mail: irpl@colis.com

JAPAN
Eastern Book Service
3-13 Hongo 3-chome, Bunkyo-ku
Tokyo 113
Tel: (81 3) 3818-0861
Fax: (81 3) 3818-0864
E-mail: orders@svt-ebs.co.jp

KENYA
Africa Book Service (E.A.) Ltd.
Quaran House, Mfangano Street
P.O. Box 45245
Nairobi
Tel: (254 2) 223 641
Fax: (254 2) 330 272

KOREA, REPUBLIC OF
Daejon Trading Co. Ltd.
P.O. Box 34, Youida, 706 Seoun Bldg
44-6 Youido-Dong, Yeongchengpo-Ku
Seoul
Tel: (82 2) 785-1631/4
Fax: (82 2) 784-0315

LEBANON
Librairie du Liban
Beirut
Tel: (961 9) 217 944
Fax: (961 9) 217 434

MALAYSIA
University of Malaya Cooperative
Bookshop, Limited
P.O. Box 1127
Jalan Pantai Baru
59700 Kuala Lumpur
Tel: (60 3) 756-5000
Fax: (60 3) 755-4424
E-mail: umkoop@tm.net.my

MEXICO
INFOTEC
Av. San Fernando No 37
Col. Toriello Guerra
14050 Mexico, D.F.
Tel: (52 5) 624-2800
Fax: (52 5) 624-2822
E-mail: infotec@rtn.net.mx
Mundi-Prensa Mexico S.A. de C.V.
c/Rio Panuco, 141-Colonia Cuauhtemoc
06500 Mexico, D.F.
Tel: (52 5) 533-5658
Fax: (52 5) 514-6799

NEPAL
Everest Media International Services (P) Ltd.
GPO Box 5443
Kathmandu
Tel: (977 1) 472 152
Fax: (977 1) 224 431

NETHERLANDS
De Lindeboom/InOr-Publikaties
P.O. Box 202, 7480 AE Haaksbergen
Tel: (31 53) 574-0004
Fax: (31 53) 572-9296
E-mail: lindeboo@worldonline.nl

NEW ZEALAND
EBSCO NZ Ltd.
Private Mail Bag 99914
New Market
Auckland
Tel: (64 9) 524-8119
Fax: (64 9) 524-8067

NIGERIA
University Press Limited
Three Crowns Building Jericho
Private Mail Bag 5095
Ibadan
Tel: (234 22) 41-1356
Fax: (234 22) 41-2056

NORWAY
NIC Info A/S
Book Department, Postboks 6512 Etterstad
N-0606 Oslo
Tel: (47 22) 97-4500
Fax: (47 22) 97-4545

PAKISTAN
Mirza Book Agency
65, Shahrah-e-Quaid-e-Azam
Lahore 54000
Tel: (92 42) 735 3601
Fax: (92 42) 576 3714
Oxford University Press
5 Bangalore Town
Sharae Faisal
PO Box 13033
Karachi-75350
Tel: (92 21) 446307
Fax: (92 21) 4547640
E-mail: oup@oup@TheOffice.net
Pak Book Corporation
Aziz Chambers 21, Queen's Road
Lahore
Tel: (92 42) 636 3222; 636 0885
Fax: (92 42) 636 2328
E-mail: pbc@brain.net.pk

PERU
Editorial Desarrollo SA
Apartado 3824, Lima 1
Tel: (51 14) 285380
Fax: (51 14) 286628

PHILIPPINES
International Booksource Center Inc.
1127-A Antipolo St, Barangay, Venezuela
Makati City
Tel: (63 2) 896 6501; 6505; 6507
Fax: (63 2) 896 1741

POLAND
International Publishing Service
Ul. Piekna 31/37
00-677 Warzawa
Tel: (48 2) 628-6089
Fax: (48 2) 621-7255
E-mail: books%ips@ikp.atm.com.pl

PORTUGAL
Livraria Portugal
Apartado 2681, Rua Do Carmo 70-74
1200 Lisbon
Tel: (1) 347-4982
Fax: (1) 347-0264

ROMANIA
Compani De Librarii Bucuresti S.A.
Str. Lipscani no. 26, sector 3
Bucharest
Tel: (40 1) 613 9645
Fax: (40 1) 312 4000

RUSSIAN FEDERATION
Isdatelstvo <Ves Mir>
9a, Kolpachniy Pereulok
Moscow 101831
Tel: (7 095) 917 87 49
Fax: (7 095) 917 92 59

SINGAPORE; TAIWAN, CHINA; MYANMAR; BRUNEI
Ashgate Publishing Asia Pacific Pte. Ltd.
41 Kallang Pudding Road #04-03
Golden Wheel Building
Singapore 349316
Tel: (65) 741-5166
Fax: (65) 742-9356
E-mail: ashgate@asianconnect.com

SLOVENIA
Gospodarski Vestnik Publishing Group
Dunajska cesta 5
1000 Ljubljana
Tel: (386 61) 133 83 47; 132 12 30
Fax: (386 61) 133 80 30
E-mail: repansekj@gvestnik.si

SOUTH AFRICA, BOTSWANA
For single titles:
Oxford University Press Southern Africa
Vasco Boulevard, Goodwood
P.O. Box 12119, N1 City 7463
Cape Town
Tel: (27 21) 595 4400
Fax: (27 21) 595 4430
E-mail: oxford@oup.co.za
For subscription orders:
International Subscription Service
P.O. Box 41095
Craighall
Johannesburg 2024
Tel: (27 11) 880-1448
Fax: (27 11) 880-6248
E-mail: iss@is.co.za

SPAIN
Mundi-Prensa Libros, S.A.
Castello 37
28001 Madrid
Tel: (34 1) 431-3399
Fax: (34 1) 575-3998
E-mail: libreria@mundiprensa.es
Mundi-Prensa Barcelona
Consell de Cent, 391
08009 Barcelona
Tel: (34 3) 488-3492
Fax: (34 3) 487-7659
E-mail: barcelona@mundiprensa.es

SRI LANKA, THE MALDIVES
Lake House Bookshop
100, Sir Chittampalam Gardiner Mawatha
Colombo 2
Tel: (94 1) 32105
Fax: (94 1) 432104
E-mail: LHL@sri.lanka.net

SWEDEN
Wennergren-Williams AB
P.O. Box 1305
S-171 25 Solna
Tel: (46 8) 705-97-50
Fax: (46 8) 27-00-71
E-mail: mail@wwi.se

SWITZERLAND
Librairie Payot Service Institutionnel
Côtes-de-Montbenon 30
1002 Lausanne
Tel: (41 21) 341-3229
Fax: (41 21) 341-3235
ADECO Van Diemen EditionsTechniques
Ch. de Lacuez 41
CH1807 Blonay
Tel: (41 21) 943 2673
Fax: (41 21) 943 3605

THAILAND
Central Books Distribution
306 Silom Road
Bangkok 10500
Tel: (66 2) 235-5400
Fax: (66 2) 237-8321

TRINIDAD & TOBAGO AND THE CARRIBBEAN
Systematics Studies Ltd.
St. Augustine Shopping Center
Eastern Main Road, St. Augustine
Trinidad & Tobago, West Indies
Tel: (868) 645-8466
Fax: (868) 645-8467
E-mail: tobe@trinidad.net

UGANDA
Gustro Ltd.
PO Box 9997, Madhvani Building
Plot 16/4 Jinja Rd.
Kampala
Tel: (256 41) 251 467
Fax: (256 41) 251 468
E-mail: gus@swiftuganda.com

UNITED KINGDOM
Microinfo Ltd.
P.O. Box 3, Alton, Hampshire GU34 2PG
England
Tel: (44 1420) 86848
Fax: (44 1420) 89889
E-mail: wbank@ukminfo.demon.co.uk
The Stationery Office
51 Nine Elms Lane
London SW8 5DR
Tel: (44 171) 873-8400
Fax: (44 171) 873-8242

VENEZUELA
Tecni-Ciencia Libros, S.A.
Centro Cuidad Comercial Tamanco
Nivel C2, Caracas
Tel: (58 2) 959 5547; 5035; 0016
Fax: (58 2) 959 5636

ZAMBIA
University Bookshop, University of Zambia
Great East Road Campus
P.O. Box 32379
Lusaka
Tel: (260 1) 252 576
Fax: (260 1) 253 952

ZIMBABWE
Academic and Baobab Books (Pvt.) Ltd.
4 Conald Road, Graniteside
P.O. Box 567
Harare
Tel: 263 4 755035
Fax: 263 4 781913